JOURNAL FOR THE STUDY OF THE OLD TESTAMENT SUPPLEMENT SERIES
168

Editors
David J.A. Clines
Philip R. Davies

Executive Editor
John Jarick

Editorial Board
Richard J. Coggins, Alan Cooper, Tamara C. Eskenazi,
J. Cheryl Exum, Robert P. Gordon, Norman K. Gottwald,
Andrew D.H. Mayes, Carol Meyers, Patrick D. Miller

JSOT Press
Sheffield

THE COMPOSITION OF THE BOOK OF PROVERBS

R.N. Whybray

Journal for the Study of the Old Testament
Supplement Series 168

For David and Heather

Copyright © 1994 Sheffield Academic Press

Published by JSOT Press
JSOT Press is an imprint of
Sheffield Academic Press Ltd
343 Fulwood Road
Sheffield S10 3BP
England

Typeset by Sheffield Academic Press
and
Printed on acid-free paper in Great Britain
by Bookcraft Ltd
Midsomer Norton, Bath

British Library Cataloguing in Publication Data

A catalogue record for this book is available
from the British Library

ISBN 1-85075-457-8

CONTENTS

The book of Proverbs is a compendium of Israelite wisdom texts which, unlike the other two Old Testament books generally reckoned as wisdom books (Job and Ecclesiastes) expresses a general confidence that human society is governed by rules of conduct which can be relied on and which, if not transgressed, will ensure to the individual a safe conduct through life. Its main concern was to impress these convictions on the minds of the young and to teach these rules to anyone who was in need of guidance and was prepared to learn.

This outlook on life was not confined to a single social class; and the book contains teaching which originated in a variety of different milieus from the royal court to the peasant's cottage, expressed in quite different styles. It is the purpose of the present study to investigate the process by which such disparate material was brought together to form a single book, and also to seek to understand the structure and character of the book in its final form.

In some respects this work builds on my earlier studies of Proverbs. The main outline of Chapter 1 is to a large extent based on my analysis of Proverbs 1–9 in *Wisdom in Proverbs: The Concept of Wisdom in Proverbs 1–9* (London: SCM Press, 1965) and in my earlier Oxford doctoral thesis (1962), and parts of Chapter 2 have been adumbrated in my commentary (*Proverbs* [New Century Bible; London: Marshall Pickering; Grand Rapids: Eerdmans, 1994]) and in an article, 'Thoughts on the Composition of Proverbs 10–29', in E. Ulrich *et al.* (eds.), in *Priests, Prophets and Scribes: Essays on the Formation and Heritage of Second Temple Judaism in Honour of Joseph Blenkinsopp* (JSOTSup, 149; Sheffield: JSOT Press, 1992), pp. 102-114. In both cases, however, the material presented here represents more recent thinking and some modification of my earlier views.

No attempt is made here to provide a new commentary on the text: the sole aim is the elucidation of the process of composition of the book. In cases where the Hebrew text presents particular difficulties there are brief discussions in the notes.

Once again I am grateful to the directors of Sheffield Academic Press for the acceptance of a work of mine into the JSOT Supplement Series, and in particular to Professor David Clines for his careful work in preparing it for the press.

R.N. Whybray

ABBREVIATIONS

TRu	*Theologische Rundschau*
TynBul	*Tyndale Bulletin*
VT	*Vetus Testamentum*
VTSup	*Vetus Testamentum*, Supplements
WMANT	Wissenschaftliche Monographien zum Alten und Neuen Testament
ZAW	*Zeitschrift für die alttestamentliche Wissenschaft*

Chapter 1

PROVERBS 1–9

On the whole these chapters consist not of short, independent proverbs like those which make up most of the book, but of longer, structured poems of a quite clearly literary character.[1] The material is very varied both in form and content, and can hardly be the work of a single writer. But despite these differences, all of these chapters are marked by a common purpose: an educational one. This is all pedagogical material, designed to be used in the preparation of boys or young men to face the problems and dangers of the adult world so that they may become wise and responsible members of it.

This educational purpose is most clearly apparent in a series of ten 'lessons' or instructions put into the mouth of a parent ('your father') and addressed to his son ('my son'),[2] passages which account for more than half of the material in these chapters. In addition, there are two poems of substantial length (1.20-33; 8.1-36) in which the instruction itself ('Wisdom', ḥokmâ) comes to life and assumes the character of a

---

1. See R.N. Whybray, *Wisdom in Proverbs: The Concept of Wisdom in Proverbs 1–9* (SBT, 45; London: SCM Press, 1965). On some matters, however, my opinions have changed.

2. The question whether the terms 'father' and 'son' here are to be understood literally or whether they denote 'teacher' and 'pupil' in the context of a school has been much debated. On the existence of schools in ancient Israel, see especially R.N. Whybray, *The Intellectual Tradition in the Old Testament* (BZAW, 135; Berlin: de Gruyter, 1974), pp. 33-43; B. Lang, 'Schule und Unterricht im alten Israel', in M. Gilbert (ed.), *La sagesse de l'Ancien Testament* (BETL, 51; Gembloux: Duculot; Leuven: Leuven University Press, 1979), pp. 186-201; A. Lemaire, *Les écoles et la formation de la Bible dans l'ancien Israël* (OBO, 39; Freiburg [Switzerland]: Editions universitaires; Göttingen: Vanderhoeck & Ruprecht, 1981); F.W. Golka, 'Die israelitische Weisheitsschule oder "des Kaisers neue Kleider"', *VT* 33 (1983), pp. 257-71. For the purpose of the present study this is not a question of great importance.

woman teacher who takes up her position in the public places of the city and addresses an audience, appealing to them to recognize her inestimable qualities and to allow her to guide their lives. There is also a further, shorter poem praising Wisdom in the third person (3.13-20). In addition to the ten instructions there is also some miscellaneous teaching material (especially 6.1-19; 9.7-12). The nine chapters are framed by a preface or prologue (1.1-7) and an appendix (ch. 9) which dramatically presents two contrasting tableaux depicting two female figures, Wisdom and Folly, between whom the young pupil must choose, the one offering life and the other offering illicit enjoyment which will in reality lead to death.

The similarities and differences between these types of material are interesting and important, as are also the origins of the ideas they express and the imagery which they employ. To explore these matters is not, however, the primary purpose of this study, which is concerned only with the undoubtedly complex history of the composition of the book. Other aspects of these chapters will be discussed only in so far as they are relevant to this question. One preliminary comment on contents is, however, relevant here: apart from their generally educational character, which pervades the whole of the book of Proverbs, these chapters have common characteristics which mark them off sharply from the rest of the book and give them a kind of unity. Formally, apart from a few short passages, they are not the result of the juxtaposition of individual short proverbs but consist of carefully composed literary compositions of greater length; thematically, perhaps partly because of their greater length which permitted a fuller treatment of topics, they manifest much more integrated patterns of thought than the individual proverbs.

The Ten Instructions

The identification of these originally independent poems was first made by Whybray[3] and has been widely accepted by scholars.[4] Most

---

3. R.N. Whybray, 'The Concept of Wisdom in Proverbs I–IX' (DPhil thesis, Oxford, 1992); *Wisdom in Proverbs* (SBT, 45; London: SCM Press, 1965); 'Some Literary Problems in Proverbs I–IX', *VT* 16 (1966), pp. 482-96.

4. In *Wisdom in Proverbs* (pp. 61-71) I argued that they were deeply influenced by the Egyptian genre of wisdom literature known as the 'Instruction'. C. Kayatz (*Studien zu Proverbien 1–9* [WMANT, 22; Neukirchen–Vluyn:

of them are not in their original form, but have been augmented for various reasons, theological and non-theological. The clearest indication of their identity as a distinct literary type is that they all begin in a similar way: 1.8-9; 2.1, 9; 3.1-4; 3.21-22; 4.1-2; 4.10-12; 4.20-22; 5.1-2; 6.20-22; 7.1-3. These introductory verses have the following common characteristics:

1. They are all addressed to 'my son' ('sons' in 4.1) as the first or second word.
2. They all command the pupil to 'hear', 'receive', 'not forget', and so on, the instruction which follows (a conditional form is used in 2.1).
3. They all assert the personal authority of the speaker: the 'father' or teacher.
4. They all assert or imply the great value and utility of the father's words.
5. There is no reference to any authority beyond that of the father himself ('God and man' in 3.4 is merely a set phrase indicating universality).
6. The word 'wisdom', which occurs only twice (5.1; 4.11), here means ordinary human wisdom and is not treated—in contrast to its use elsewhere in these chapters—as a word of special significance.

The points at which the instructions concluded are more difficult to determine than are their beginnings. In several instances a verse or a short group of verses (1.19; 2.21-22; 3.53; 4.18-19; 5.21-23), which speaks in general terms of the respective fates of the wicked and/or the righteous, appears to mark a conclusion, but this is not necessarily the conclusion of the *original* instruction: expansions of earlier material in biblical books, where they occur, often tend to be placed in final positions.

Neukirchener Verlag, 1966], pp. 26-75) confirmed this view after making a detailed comparison. We both, however, emphasized that there are also important differences both of form and substance between the Egyptian and the Old Testament texts. I still recognize that the instructions in Prov. 1–9 are examples of an international genre of which the best extant non-Israelite examples are Egyptian, but would now prefer to speak of parallel developments rather than of 'influence'. Although there are structural as well as thematic parallels with the Egyptian texts, the question of the composition of the instructions in Prov. 1–9 is a complex one which can only be discussed on the basis of internal evidence.

Proverbs 1.8-19 and 4.20-27

The instruction in its simplest form as it occurs in these chapters is observable in 1.8-19 and 4.20-27. In these two cases the extent of the instruction is clearly marked out, since the surrounding material is incontrovertibly extraneous to it. Prov. 1.8-19 is immediately preceded by the Prologue (1.1-7), and immediately followed by the first of the wisdom poems in which Wisdom, not the human teacher, speaks (1.20-33); 4.20-27 is similarly circumscribed, as it follows a previous instruction (4.10-19) and precedes the introductory verse of another (5.1).

These two instructions are particularly illuminating because they exemplify this type of teaching medium in its simplest and most characteristic form. After the introductory verses urging the pupil to pay attention to the speaker's words on the grounds of the immense benefits which will accrue from this, each makes its point clearly and simply. There is, however, no rigid conformity here to a fixed formula; each instruction puts its message in its own way. Prov. 1.8-19 describes a hypothetical temptation scene ('My child, if...', v. 10) in which a band of young ruffians attempts to lead the pupil into crime, and ends with a prohibition ('my child, do not walk in their way', v. 15) accompanied by a warning of the appalling consequences of crime: 'it takes away the life of its possessors' (v. 19).[5] The lesson of 4.20-27, on the other hand, is conveyed in a series of imperatives or commands requiring moral behaviour.

Despite the difference in teaching method it is important to notice the strong similarities between these two instructions. In both cases the teaching is given by and on the sole authority of the human father or teacher; the word 'wisdom' does not occur, and the pupil is not urged to embrace or take to heart any abstract principle or personified divine attribute, as elsewhere in these chapters. It is also to be noted that there is no mention of God in either of these instructions, either as teacher or as guarantor of a cosmic order. While it would be mistaken to describe these two instructions as 'secular teaching', it is fair to conclude that what we have here is a pair of straightforward

---

5.   It is not entirely correct to say that no additions have been made to this instruction. Verse 16 is almost identical with Isa. 59.7a, and has almost certainly been copied from there. It is missing from the best manuscripts of LXX, and is a gloss probably added in order to stress the heinousness of the criminal activity being proposed.

lessons taught by a wholly authoritative human father to a young son. Prov. 1.8-19 consists of twelve poetical couplets, 4.20-27 of eight.

In view of the simplicity and elegant compactness of these two instructions, it is reasonable to analyse the remaining eight, some of which are much more complex and diffuse, in order to discover whether there is evidence of a pattern, and whether additional material may have been attached to them which obscures a simpler form similar to that of those discussed above.

Proverbs 2.1-22

Chapter 2 is an extreme case of compositional complexity.[6] In MT its twenty-two verses comprise a single sentence, but one which contains a multiplicity of subordinate clauses. It begins, like the other instructions, with the words 'My son...'; but unlike all the others, which employ the imperative command at this point, it employs the conditional mode: not, for instance, 'My son, accept my words' but 'My son, *if* you accept my words...' Otherwise v. 1 corresponds closely to the opening words of the other instructions; but vv. 2-4, which continue the conditional sentence with a series of clauses parallel with those of v. 1, qualify the 'my words' and 'my commandments' of the teacher, equating them with wisdom (*ḥokmâ*) and two synonyms, *bînâ* and *tᵉbûnâ*, this 'wisdom' being, according to v. 4, so precious a commodity that it must be sought for like silver or hidden treasures. This language takes the reader a long way from the initial call in v. 1 to the pupil to receive (*lāqaḥ*) and cherish (*ṣāpan*) the teacher's words, for those are readily available to the pupil and do not need to be sought (*biqqēš*) and searched for (*ḥāpaś*) as if they were difficult to find.

Now with v. 5 comes the first apodosis in this extremely complicated sentence: '*then* you will understand...' But this verse and those which follow now introduce yet a third goal for the pupil. They speak neither of the teacher's words nor of wisdom: the object to be obtained is now the understanding of the fear of Yahweh and the knowledge of God; but this, in the terms of the sentence as a whole, must be understood as identical with, or at least as closely associated with, both the teacher's words and 'wisdom'. Verses 1-5 taken as a whole assert that paying attention to the teacher is to be attentive to

---

6. For fuller details see Whybray, 'Some Literary Problems'.

wisdom, and that if the pupil seeks for wisdom he will also attain to the fear and knowledge of God. As has already been remarked, none of these thoughts is to be found in either 1.8-19 or 4.20-27.

The apodosis in v. 5 is followed in v. 6 by a pair of explanatory or motive-clauses (*kî*, 'For...'). The understanding of the fear of Yahweh will be obtained *because* he is the source of the wisdom spoken of in vv. 2-4. Verses 7-8 continue this theme, adding a new ethical note: Yahweh's wisdom is available only to the upright (*y^{e}šārîm*) and the blameless (*hōl^{e}kê tōm*), when it will protect the ways of justice (*mišpāṭ*) and of his faithful ones (*ḥ^{a}sîdâw*).

There then follows in vv. 9-11 a second and parallel apodosis. Verse 9 begins with an exact repetition of the first words of v. 5: 'then you will understand...' ('*āz tābîn*); but now the reference to Yahweh is dropped, and in vv. 10-11 wisdom is again the object of attention. The ethical note—righteousness (*ṣedeq*), justice (*mišpāṭ*) and uprightness (*mêšārîm*)—is retained in v. 9; but in the motive-clauses (again *kî*, 'for...') in vv. 10-11 this moral sense is to be the consequence of the activity of a semi-personified wisdom who— together with a number of synonymous abstract qualities—is the subject of the verbs: she will enter the pupil's will (*lēb*), give him delight, and protect him.

Verses 12-15 and 16-19 are again parallel passages, both beginning with the same words, *l^{e}haṣṣîl^{e}kā min-*, 'to save you from...' The first of these passages (vv. 12-15) is expressed in extremely general terms: the pupil will be saved by wisdom from the 'way of evil', specifically from wicked persons whose character and activities are described in general terms in a series of clauses.

It is to be observed that up to this point (v. 15) the chapter has dealt entirely in generalities or abstractions. No specific conduct is prescribed or warned against, as, for example, in 1.8-19 (a warning against joining a gang and committing acts of violence). The language is very repetitive: for example, *ḥokmâ* and its equivalents occur eleven times in these verses and words for 'way' or 'path' nine times. These generalities are in essence nothing more than a lengthy elaboration of the introductory words of the father in v. 1; but they have the function of introducing references both to a semi-personified wisdom and to Yahweh as the source of that wisdom.

It is only when we come to vv. 16-19 that a concrete piece of advice is given to the pupil: a warning against the '*iššâ zārâ*, the 'foreign woman' or more probably 'the wife of another man',[7] that is, an adulteress, association with whom leads to 'death'. This passage is clearly the original core of the instruction. It closely resembles, even to the use of the same or similar words and phrases, the central admonition of three other instructions which have the same theme (5.3ff.; 6.24ff.; 7.5, 25-27). This supports the view that we are here dealing with an originally brief instruction to which the lengthy elaboration in terms of a personified wisdom and of Yahweh's relationship to wisdom (vv. 2-11) and also the vague reference to rescue from evildoers (vv. 12-15) have been added.

The chapter ends in vv. 20-22 with a general admonition to be good (v. 20) and an equally general depiction of the contrasting fates of the righteous (v. 21) and the wicked (v. 22). These are generalities similar to those of vv. 12-15, and may have been added to the original instruction by the same hand. It is difficult to determine whether they are original to the instruction or not, because these instructions have no fixed type of conclusion: four of them, at any rate in their present form, end with similar generalities (1.19; 3.32-35; 4.18-19; 5.21-23), although there also the question of originality arises. On the other hand, in the other five instructions (3.1ff.; 4.1ff.; 4.20ff.; 6.20ff.; 7.1ff.) there are no comparable concluding verses: they end with the completion of their main admonitions. In the case of 2.20-22 there is a further point which suggests, probably conclusively, that these verses are a later addition or additions to the original instruction: v. 20 is syntactically only very loosely attached to what precedes. Its opening words, *l^ema'an tēlēk*, 'so that you may walk', cannot be the continuation of v. 19, which is not an address to the pupil but is a general statement in the third person plural about the fate of those who are seduced by the adulteress.

Once the additional material has been set aside, the outlines of the original instruction can be discerned. It consists of a simple sentence.

7. The recent commentaries are undecided on this point. I accept the view of P. Humbert, 'La "femme étrangère" du Livre des Proverbes', *RES* 6 (1937), pp. 49-64; 'Les adjectifs "zâr" et "nokrî" et la "femme étrangère" des proverbes bibliques', in *Mélanges syriens offerts à M. René Dussaud* (Paris: Paul Geuthner, 1939), I, pp. 259-66 = *Opuscules d'un hébraisant* (Neuchâtel: Delachaux & Niestlé, 1958), pp. 111-18. The view of L.A. Snijders, 'The Meaning of *zār* in the Old Testament', *OTS* 10 (1954), pp. 63ff. that the reference is to the wife of an 'outsider' or outcast is less convincing.

The introductory section in which the father commends his own teaching was originally quite brief (cf. 1.8-19). Formally it consisted of a simple conditional sentence: 'If...then...' (*'im ...'āz*). The expanded instruction in its present form has a triple protasis (*'im* occurs in vv. 1, 3 and 4) and two apodoses (*'āz* occurs twice, in vv. 5 and 9). The simplest and most probably original form of the introductory section would have consisted merely of vv. 1 and 9. In those verses the pupil is simply told that by attending to his father's teaching he will acquire knowledge of righteous conduct. There then followed the main part of the instruction, which consisted, as suggested above, not of the first statement of motive (vv. 11-15) but of the second (vv. 16-19). Whether vv. 20-22 constituted the original conclusion or whether the instruction ended with v. 19 is not certain (but probably the latter).

The length of the original instruction thus reconstructed (six couplets [or possibly nine]) may be compared with that of the two instructions already considered. Prov. 1.8-19 has twelve and 4.20-27 eight. It should be noted that the original syntax of this instruction lent itself particularly readily to expansion. Each syntactical element— protasis, apodosis, motive-clause, final clause ('to save you...') has been simply duplicated or even tripled with identically constructed clauses, so producing a longer and seriously overloaded sentence, but one which yet retains its syntactical and logical correctness.

Proverbs 3.1-12

This instruction also is delimited by what precedes and what follows: that is, by the previous instruction and by the wisdom poem of vv. 13-20. In the introduction (vv. 1-4), which corresponds to the introductions to the other instructions, the father commends his own teaching, promising that obedience to it will ensure longevity and favour with God and people (the first line of v. 3 is an intrusion);[8] the contents of this teaching are however wholly concerned with the pupil's relationship with Yahweh. The body of the instruction (vv. 5-10) comprises three admonitions each consisting of two couplets and

---

8.   Verse 3, unusually, contains three lines. LXX lacks the third; but in view of the parallels in 1.9 and 3.22 it is more probable that the 'them' of lines two and three refers to the father's 'commandments' of v. 1 rather than to the 'loyalty and faithfulness (*ḥesed wĕʾĕmet*)' of the first line, which is redundant.

expressed as imperatives, advocating a humble attitude towards him—trust, fear, sacrificial offerings—and promising, in return, success in life, good health and material wealth. Only vv. 11-12, which constitute a fourth admonition, appear to be a later addition to this instruction: these verses are concerned not with duties towards God but with the pupil's proper reaction to God's actions towards him. Without them the instruction comprises ten couplets.

As will be demonstrated below, this is the only one of the ten instructions in these chapters in which, in its original form, the teaching is concerned with God. The reason for this is not clear. One possibility is that it was added to the collection, perhaps at a stage before additions of this kind had been made to others of the instructions, by an author or editor who considered avoidance of 'God-talk' to be a serious omission from the educational curriculum; another possible explanation is that the subject of duties towards God *was* recognized in the circles which produced these instructions, but that it was regarded as only one among many suitable educational themes, best confined to a single instruction, when it could be dealt with at length.

A feature which is wholly absent from this instruction is the theme of wisdom ('Do not be wise in your own eyes' in v. 7 is a standard warning in Proverbs; there is no occurrence of the word *ḥokmâ* or its equivalents here, and no admonition to embrace wisdom). But it may well be significant that the poem which immediately follows (vv. 13-18) is entirely concerned with the commendation and praise of a semi-personified wisdom: in other words, that the wisdom poem may have been deliberately selected by an editor to remedy that omission.

Proverbs 3.21-35

This instruction has undergone considerable expansion. It may originally have consisted of vv. 21-24, 27-31 (nine couplets). Verses 21-24 form the introduction, although v. 21 presents some textual difficulties. First, its two lines, apart from the first word *beni*, 'My son', appear to have been reversed; this is shown by the fact that the third person plural verb *'al-yālūzû*, 'let them not escape', has no antecedent and so no discernible subject. The reference is clearly to the nouns mentioned in the second line which originally came first, namely 'sound wisdom' (*tūšiyyâ*) and 'prudence' (*mezimmâ*). Secondly, in MT this introduction differs from that of the other instructions in that the father in his address to his son does not state that it is his own teaching to which he is referring (contrast, e.g., '*my* words', '*my* commandments', 2.1 and parallels). This may, of course, be implied; but it is interesting that LXX has '*my* counsel and understanding' here. Apart from this, vv. 21-24 correspond to the introductions to the other instructions: adherence to these principles will confer 'life' (cf. 3.2; 4.22), 'adornment' (*ḥēn*) for the neck (cf. 3.3) and security (vv. 23-24; cf. 6.22).

Verses 25-26 comprise a negative admonition with motive-clause. These verses are probably an addition to the original instruction, made in order to equate obedience to the father's teaching with trust in Yahweh. Verse 25 taken by itself is redundant: it merely repeats the theme of the previous verses; its function is to prepare for v. 26. Verse 26 unexpectedly introduces Yahweh for the first time, asserting that the source of the pupil's wellbeing, on which he may safely rely, is not simply the practice of the principles instilled into him by the father but Yahweh himself: it is he who will see to it that he does not stumble, a promise already made in v. 23 with regard to the father's teaching.

The body of the instruction (vv. 27-31) is quite simple in structure. It consists of five negative admonitions each forming a single couplet, setting out principles of conduct towards neighbours, on prompt repayment of debts, and on refraining from hostile intentions and actions. It may therefore be seen as a counterpart to 3.1-10, which is concerned with duties towards God. There is no further mention of Yahweh here: this is straightforward social teaching. Verses 32-35, however, are of a quite different kind. Verses 32-34 contain no specific teaching but speak in quite general terms of the contrasting fates of the righteous and humble on the one hand and of the wicked on the other, entirely in the manner of many of the individual proverbs in chs. 10–29. They also serve to reintroduce a reference to Yahweh as the judge of human conduct who rewards the righteous and the wicked in the appropriate manner. These verses are almost certainly secondary, as also is the final verse, v. 35, which also has close affinities with the proverbs of the later chapters but differs from vv. 32-34 in that the contrast which it makes is between wise (*ḥᵃkāmîm*) and fools (*kᵉsîlîm*) rather than righteous and wicked and so makes the only reference to wisdom in this instruction.

Proverbs 4.1-9
This instruction in its present form is delimited by the instructions which immediately precede and follow it. It differs from the others in that the main section consists of the father's reminiscence of the teaching which his own father had given him when he was a child— teaching which he clearly sees as equally appropriate to the education of his own son.

The introduction (vv. 1-2), apart from the use of the plural 'sons' (*bānîm*) in place of the usual 'my son', corresponds to the introductions to the other instructions. The main section, quoting the words of the speaker's own father, comprises vv. 3-4, 5b with the exception of the final word of v. 4 ('and live'); v. 5a is also an intrusion. These intruded words are lacking in LXX. That the text of MT is dislocated is shown by the fact that v. 4 has three lines instead of the usual two. Originally v. 4b (apart from 'and live') together with v. 5b formed a single couplet: 'Keep my commandments, forget them not, and do not turn away from the words of my mouth'. Verse 5a, 'Get wisdom, get insight', anticipates v. 7, of which it is a shortened form.

Versus 7-9 are an originally separate short poem on the need to embrace a personified wisdom; this has been attached to the main body of the instruction, which originally consisted of five couplets (vv. 1-4 plus the couplet reconstructed above on the basis of LXX). The additions to it are entirely concerned with wisdom: there is no reference to Yahweh. It is possible that this instruction was originally longer.

Proverbs 4.10-19
This instruction also is delimited by the previous and following instructions. Its main body of teaching (vv. 14-19), which includes an appropriate general conclusion (vv. 18-19), is a warning in general terms (contrasting in this respect with 10-16) against associating with the wicked. Like several others, it contains no reference to wisdom and none to Yahweh. The introductory verses (vv. 10-13), however, show signs of expansion. Verses 10 and 12 correspond closely to the original introductions to other instructions: the father commends his teaching to his son and promises (v. 10b) that it will confer longevity on him. This promise of life (or long life) is found also in 3.2 and 3.22 (3.2 uses the same phrase *šᵉnôt ḥayyîm*, 'years of life'). Secondly, the father promises that obedience to his teaching will

ensure that in his progress through life the pupil's step will not be hampered and he will not stumble. The same metaphor is employed in 3.23 (compare also 6.22). It is significant that in those other instructions these promises follow immediately on the initial commendation by the father of his own teaching, so that they are represented as the direct consequences of obedience to it. Here, however, the pattern is broken: the promises are separated from the initial commendation by a reference to wisdom; the father claims to have taught his son 'in the way of wisdom' (v. 11). This puts the matter in a new light, suggesting that it is this acquisition of wisdom that guarantees the promises.

There is thus reason to suppose that v. 11 is an interpolation into the original instruction; and this hypothesis is strengthened by v. 13, which picks up that verse with a recommendation to 'hold on to' and 'guard' instruction (*mûsār*, which is here an obvious equivalent of *hokmâ*, since it is treated here—and nowhere else in the Old Testament—as a feminine noun!) This *mûsār* is here personified and stated to be 'your life'. This is a clear case of a reinterpretation which makes wisdom rather than the father's teaching the source of the pupil's happiness and success.

The original instruction, then, consisted of vv. 10, 12, 14-19 (eight couplets). It should be noted also that there is no reference to Yahweh in the entire instruction.[9]

Proverbs 5.1-23

This instruction and the two which follow it (chs. 6 and 7) have the same theme: the avoidance of the temptation of the adulteress and the evil consequences of yielding to it—a theme already treated in 2.1-22. All these have been extensively expanded.[10]

Verses 1 and 2 of this chapter appear to be the introduction to the

9.   Verses 18 and 19 have apparently been accidentally reversed. Putting the latter before the former avoids two abrupt changes of subject.

10.   J.E. Goldingay, 'Proverbs V and IX', *RB* 84 (1977), pp. 80-87, postulates a three-stage development of the chapter, the clue to which is to be found in the three occurrences of the verb *šāgâ* (usually rendered by 'to go astray') in vv. 19, 20 and 23. This argument is somewhat contrived. A further weakness of Goldingay's position is that he underestimates the importance of the basic pattern shared by the instructions in these chapters in their original form, mistakenly seeing vv. 7, 15 and 20 as the beginnings of new instructions comparable with vv. 1-6, 8.

instruction, though v. 2 is difficult and no satisfactory solution has emerged.[11] In v. 1 the father, in commending his teaching, describes it as '*my* wisdom' (*ḥokmātî*) and '*my* understanding' (*tᵉbûnātî*); this is the only passage in these instructions where this is so, although in 4.11 the father claims to teach his son 'in the way of wisdom' (*bᵉderek ḥokmâ*; no possessive pronoun). There is, however, no further reference in this instruction to wisdom (contrast the elaborate development in ch. 2), and the word is used here simply as one of the many synonyms for the parental teaching which are employed in the introductions to the instructions. But its use as a description of the father's teaching here and in 4.11 may have constituted the starting-point for the subsequent development of the theme.

Although wisdom is not a major theme here, this instruction has been expanded to become a kind of repository for miscellaneous matter concerned with marital fidelity and the folly of extramarital sexual activity that originally had no connection with the particular warning given to the pupil against the temptations of the adulteress, which constituted the main body of the instruction in its original form.

This main body consisted of vv. 3-6, 8 (v. 7, which is virtually identical with 7.24, is an interpolation intended to add emphasis to the warning which follows in v. 8). These verses, which speak of the honeyed speech of the adulteress (here simply called *zārâ*, literally 'stranger [woman]'; elsewhere more fully '*iššâ zārâ* [*ēšet rā'*, 'woman of evil', in 6.24]), of her leading her victims to their death, and of a specific warning to keep away from her house, correspond closely, and to a considerable extent verbally, with the central passages of the three parallel instructions (2.16-19; 6.24-25 [cf. v. 32]; 7.5, 25-27). However, one item common to the others is lacking: the introductory line 'To keep/save you from the strange woman/woman of evil' (cf. 2.16a, 6.24a, 7.5a and parallels in the second lines of those verses). This omission is almost certainly accidental and should be restored after v. 2; otherwise the transition from the introductory verses is too abrupt.

The remainder of the chapter is characterized by differences of style, language and point of view. Verses 9-14 are concerned not with

11. A literal translation would be: 'in keeping discretion (*lišmōr mᵉzimmôt*), and knowledge of your lips let them/they will guard (*yinṣᵉrû*)'.

seduction but with the fate of the adulterer: not the inexperienced, unmarried boy or young man but the unfaithful married man who courts disgrace and condemnation by the 'assembled congregation' of citizens. There is no mention of his suffering 'death'; rather, he will fall into the hands of an outraged husband and his family, to his financial ruin (vv. 9-11). Verses 15-20 are also addressed to a married man, exhorting him to marital fidelity. Verses 21-23 may contain elements of the original conclusion to the instruction: they are expressed in general terms and in the third person, and might be relevant either to the case of the erring young man or to that of the adulterer. Verse 21 contains the only reference to Yahweh in the chapter: he is represented as arbiter and assessor of all human conduct. Apart from 'my wisdom' in v. 1 the theme of wisdom does not occur at all.

Proverbs 6.20-35

This instruction is preceded by material external to the series (6.1-19) and followed by the final instruction in the series (7.1ff.). The introduction (vv. 20-22)[12] has the same features as the corresponding introductions (cf. especially 1.8, 9; 3.1-4; 3.21-23; 4.10, 12). Verse 23 is also intended to be part of the introduction rather than of the main body of the instruction, but is a later addition. Its first line is a gloss on v. 20, reinterpreting *miṣwâ*, 'commandment' and *tôrâ*, 'teaching' in that verse—terms frequently used in these chapters of the father's teaching—in terms of a later Jewish wisdom connected with the Mosaic Law. It has the form of an explanatory gloss ('x is y'), and it also interrupts the sequence in which protection from the temptations of the adulteress is said to be the direct consequence of the father's teaching. The second line appears to expand the thought of the first while using words appropriate to the context, so completing the couplet.

Like 5.1ff., this instruction has been expanded with secondary material concerning the folly of unchastity. The direct address which

---

12. Verse 22, however, may originally have been a reference to Wisdom from which an initial line (e.g. 'Say to Wisdom, "you are my sister"', cf. 7.4a) has dropped out, and so additional to the original instruction. The difficulty lies in the fact that the verbs in this verse are feminine singular when plural forms would be expected. The fact that the verse has three lines in MT is an additional reason for suspicion of the present text.

forms the body of the instruction ends with v. 25, and is succeeded by a series of general statements in the third person. In v. 26 the woman is no longer called *'iššâ zārâ* and *nokriyyâ* (or *'ēšet rā'*, as in v. 24), but *'iššâ zônâ*, 'prostitute' and *'ēšet 'îš*, 'a man's wife', phrases never used elsewhere in these instructions. Again, as in 5.9-14, the penalty for such behaviour is not 'death' as in the other instructions, but financial ruin, dishonour and physical violence inflicted by the wronged husband.

It is possible, however, that some small part of vv. 26-35 belonged to the original instruction. If so, v. 32 may fill that role: it has the character of a general conclusion, although it is not clear what is meant by *mašḥît napšô*, literally, 'destroys himself'. It has been suggested that v. 35 is also original since it resumes the second person address: *kî tarbeh šōḥad*, '(even) though *you* offer a large bribe'; but this is less likely.

The additions to the instruction are, then, extensive. It originally consisted of vv. 20-22 (or 20-21) and possibly also v. 32 (four couplets or possibly five, plus a triplet [v. 22]). There is no reference to wisdom either in the original instruction or in the additional material (though see n. 12) and none to God.

Proverbs 7.1-27

This is the tenth and final instruction in the series, and the fourth of the warnings against the adulteress. Like the others, it has been greatly expanded, but most of the additional material is of a somewhat different kind from that found elsewhere: a complete and originally independent poem on a similar subject but in a completely different style has been inserted into it (vv. 6-23).[13]

The introduction consists of vv. 1-3. As with 6.23, however, an intrusive verse (v. 4) has been inserted between the introduction and the main body, which begins with the words 'to keep you from the adulteress *(mē' iššâ zārâ)*' (cf. 2.16; 6.24). This insertion is somewhat different in character from 6.23: it is a recommendation to the pupil to adopt a personified wisdom as a close friend or to take her as his bride (literally, 'sister'). This is the only reference to wisdom in the chapter.

13. For a more detailed analysis of this chapter see Whybray, 'Some Literary Problems', pp. 482-86.

Verses 6-23 are a complete story, now connected with what precedes by the particle *kî*, 'for', at the beginning of v. 6. The main body of the original instruction, which began in v. 5, is resumed in vv. 25-27. Verse 24 reiterates the father's call for attention to his words already made in v. 1 with the word *wᵉ'attâ*, 'And now', an indication that there has been a digression and that it is necessary to resume the interrupted address to the pupil. Verses 25-27 complete the instruction with a warning to avoid association with the adulteress, which will lead to 'death'; these verses correspond closely to 2.18-19 and 5.5.

Verses 6-23 constitute a self-contained literary unit with its own introduction and conclusion. Although its theme is similar to that of the instruction into which it has been inserted, it is a vivid and polished moral story of a literary type quite distinct from it, depending for its effect on the vividness of its descriptions and giving in detail the words with which the woman seduces the young man, her appearance, and the setting: features which are only mentioned very briefly in the original instruction. Moreover, features which are entirely lacking in the instruction play a prominent part here: the sacrificial feast and the absence of the woman's husband. This is a narrative lacking an address by the narrator to the young man, and the moral is implicit rather than explicit: the dangers are clearly pointed out, but there is no warning as such. The narrative form describing a scene observed by the narrator has no parallels in these chapters.

The original instruction, then, consisted of vv. 1-3, 5, 25-27, seven couplets in all. Wisdom is mentioned only in v. 4, and there is no mention of God in the chapter.

Conclusion

The above analyses yield the following data. (1) These chapters contain ten instructions addressed by a father to a son. (2) Of these, eight have undergone subsequent expansion. They originally consisted of 2.1, 9, 16-19; 3.1-2, 3bc, 4-10; 3.21-24, 27-31; 4.1-4, 5b; 4.10, 12, 14-19; 5.1-6, 8; 6.20-22, 24-25 (32); 7.1-3, 5, 25-27. Prov. 1.8-19 and 4.20-27 have not been expanded. (3) Some of the expansions were made for non-theological and non-ideological reasons: for example, in chs. 5, 6 and 7 material has been added in order to assemble various warnings about the consequences of sexual irregularity under a single heading. Several instructions, however, have been expanded by the addition of material which associates the father's teaching with a personified wisdom or with Yahweh:

a. In one case (2.1ff.) additions of both kinds have been made.
b. In three[14] cases (4.1ff.; 4.10ff.; 7.1ff.) references to a personified Wisdom have been added, but none to Yahweh.
c. In three cases (3.1ff.; 3.21ff.; 5.1ff.) references to Yahweh have been added, but none to a personified Wisdom.
d. In three cases (1.8ff; 4.20ff.; 6.20ff.) there are no references either to a personified Wisdom or to Yahweh.
e. It may be significant that, if the arrangement of chs. 1–9 as a whole is taken into account, three of the instructions are immediately followed by poems which are concerned both with personified Wisdom and with Yahweh: thus 1.8-19 is followed by 1.20ff.; 3.1-12 by 3.13-20; 7.1-27 by ch. 8.
f. The fact that two of the original instructions (1.8-19 and 4.20-27) are simple examples of the father's teaching to which nothing has been added tends to confirm the view that this was a standard type of instruction to which the other eight corresponded in their original form.
g. The analysis is also supported by the comparative uniformity of the length of the postulated original instructions, which ranges from five to twelve couplets, compared with a range of eight to twenty-three couplets for the instructions in their augmented form.

The subjects dealt with in the original instructions and the order in which they are arranged makes it improbable that they ever constituted a 'book', whether a handbook for teachers or a textbook for students, though they clearly belong to the same literary genre and have a common purpose: the instruction of the young. Four out of the ten have precisely the same theme—warning against association with the adulteress—and in their present arrangement three of these are bunched together at the end of the series, while the other stands near the beginning. It is extremely unlikely that there should have been such repetition in the practical handbook, especially since all four employ similar, sometimes identical, language. Two (1.8ff. and 4.10ff.) deal with the subject of participation in violent behaviour.

14. Or four: see note 12 above.

Prov. 3.1ff. is the only one which is concerned with God and what is due to him; it is possible that the fact that 3.21ff., on duties towards neighbours, comes next in the series, although in the final arrangement of the chapters the poem on wisdom (3.13-20) now comes between them.

A number of attempts have been made to find a logical system in the arrangement of the instructions in their present form. Scott, Plöger and Meinhold[15] consider that ch. 2 was composed as an introduction to the following chapters, setting out the themes to be treated and the programme to be carried out in chs. 4–7. Lang,[16] however, maintains that it is useless to seek for a structure here, citing Egyptian instructions and also Ecclesiasticus as indicative of the indifference of the authors of ancient Near Eastern works to this kind to structure. In fact, those who have argued for a logical sequence of themes in these chapters have failed to establish their case.

The large number of the instructions gathered in these chapters suggests that there was in ancient Israel at some time (there is no clear evidence of date, and the range of dates proposed by modern scholars ranges from the tenth to the third centuries BC) a distinct literary type of educational treatise, of which they are examples. The close similarity between them, especially in the form and language of the introductory sections, may suggest that some have been modelled on others, although there is, as far as can be seen, no way of discovering which of them have the priority. The question why these originally independent texts were subsequently put together to form part of what are now chs. 1–9 will be considered at a later stage in this study.

The reasons for the augmentation of most of the instructions with material concerned with a personified Wisdom and/or with Yahweh must now be considered.

15. R.B.Y. Scott, *Proverbs/Ecclesiastes* (AB, 18; New York: Doubleday, 1965), p. 16; O. Plöger, *Sprüche Salomos (Proverbia)* (BKAT, 17; Neukirchen–Vluyn: Neukirchener Verlag, 1984), p. 5; A. Meinhold, *Die Sprüche. I. Sprüche Kapitel 1–15* (Zürcher Kommentare AT, 16.1; Zürich: Theologischer Verlag, 1991), p. 43.

16. B. Lang, *Die weisheitliche Lehrrede: Eine Untersuchung von Sprüche 1–7* (SBS, 54; Stuttgart: KBW, 1972).

The Additions to the Instructions

It is probably advisable to treat the wisdom additions and the Yahweh additions separately, even though in ch. 2, the only one of the instructions in which both types occur, the Yahweh addition (vv. 5-8) immediately follows the first wisdom addition (vv. 2-4) and the two have been deliberately connected by the phrase 'For it is Yahweh' (emphatic position) 'who gives wisdom'. But it is not clear that in general in these instructions wisdom is presented, as it were, as an intermediary between the father's teaching and Yahweh.

The fact that in three of the instructions there is no reference either to wisdom or to Yahweh, and that in all the remainder apart from ch. 2 only wisdom *or* Yahweh is mentioned shows that there has been no *systematic* editing of this kind. The additions are sporadic and unevenly distributed. A thoroughgoing redaction would not have left so much of the material untouched.

The Wisdom Additions

The depiction of Wisdom as something more than simply a human attribute but rather in the guise of a living female figure who is to be accepted as teacher and companion, embraced and loved is and remains a mysterious literary phenomenon. For some scholars[17] this is principally a literary device invented as an encouragement to the pupil to take wise teaching to heart and to reject temptation, especially in sexual matters: as a counterpart to the adulteress who appears in several of the instructions. At the other extreme, Lang[18] maintains that the figure is based on an originally divine figure, an Israelite goddess. Its origin has been sought in the Egyptian goddess Maat;[19] and the influence of other deities, Mesopotamian and Canaanite, has also been postulated.

In this study I am not primarily concerned with the origins of the figure, but rather with its function in these chapters. It is remarkable that in the Old Testament it appears only here, though it is a

17. E.g. Meinhold, *Die Sprüche*, pp. 44-45.
18. Especially *Wisdom and the Book of Proverbs: An Israelite Goddess Redefined* (New York: Pilgrim Press, 1986), *passim*.
19. E.g. by C. Kayatz, *Studien zu Proverbien 1–9* (WMANT, 22; Neukirchen–Vluyn: Neukirchener Verlag, 1966).

predominant feature in Ecclesiasticus, especially ch. 24, and was even
more fully developed in later Jewish theology. In Proverbs 1–9 it is
the main subject of the wisdom poems 1.20-33, 3.13-20 and ch. 8 (see
below). In the instructions themselves it appears only sporadically:
only in 2.2-4, 10-15; 4.5-9, 13; 7.4. There it is not defined, but is
always closely associated, and even virtually identified with, the
father's teaching. It is to be sought at all costs and to be kept and
treasured (2.3-4; 4.5, 7-8) and will become a close friend or even a
bride (7.4); it will enter the pupil's heart, will watch over him, and
will save him from harm (2.10, 11-15); it is, in fact, his 'life' (4.13).

Whether or not the figure of Wisdom in these chapters has been
influenced by mythological models, Israelite or foreign, there can be
no doubt that the authors of chs. 2 and 7 intended to present it as in
some sense an alternative to the adulteress who appears in these
chapters. The pupil is presented with a choice: he must choose
between 'life' and 'death'; and these alternatives are presented to him
in the form of two attractive 'women': Wisdom, made available to
him through the father's teaching as virtuous companion and bride,
and the adulteress, more obviously alluring but lethal. It is the need to
impress this choice on the young pupil that has prompted the addition
of these passages to the original instructions. This intention can be
seen most clearly in 7.3-5, where the admonition 'Say to wisdom,
"You are my sister [i.e. bride]"' has been interpolated (v. 4) into the
father's admonition to the pupil to heed his words because they will
'keep you from the adulteress'.

In the other two instructions in which wisdom passages occur (4.1-9
and 4.10-19) the adulteress does not appear, and no such alternative is
therefore offered. In 4.10-19 the single wisdom verse (v. 13) is
simply attached to the introductory verses commending the father's
teaching, and appears to be intended to present the alternative to a life
of violence (vv. 14-19). In 4.1-9, where the main body of the
instruction is very short (only vv. 3-4, 5b), the wisdom verses (5a, 6-
9) are probably intended to fill out an otherwise rather limping piece
of teaching; no alternative or rival attraction is mentioned at all. It has
already been suggested that this instruction may be only a fragment of
an originally fuller one; but whatever contents it may previously have
had, it remains true that both it and 4.10-19 lack the dramatic effect
produced by instructions in which *both* female figures appear as

'rivals'. Their wisdom verses are perhaps to be regarded as imitations in the same mode.

It is important to note that in all of these passages that have been added to certain instructions Wisdom, though at least partially personified, is always referred to in the third person: she does not speak. The literary relationship between these passages and the two poems 1.20-33 and ch. 8, where Wisdom is the central character and speaks at length, is a matter which concerns the composition of these chapters as a whole.

The Yahweh Additions
The paucity of Yahweh additions to the instructions is striking. Setting aside 3.1-12, where the references to Yahweh are not subsequent additions but constitute the main theme, they occur only in three instructions: 2.1-22; 3.21-35; 5.1-23. Otherwise Yahweh is not mentioned at all, either in the original text or in the supplementary material.

The only substantial Yahweh addition is 2.5-8, which immediately follows the wisdom addition in vv. 2-4. (The reference to 'the covenant of her God' in v. 17 of this chapter means no more than 'her sacred covenant', and is probably not a reference to Yahweh.) The other two, 3.26 and 5.21, are brief interpolations. Prov. 3.26 is appended to a passage commending the father's teaching (see above on that passage), offering Yahweh as a source of protection to the pupil; 5.21 introduces Yahweh as the judge of human conduct, as an alternative to the statement in v. 22 that it is the iniquities of the wicked which are the cause of their fate. It should be noted that all these verses could be removed from the text without causing any dislocation of syntax or sense.

We may conclude that there has been no systematic attempt to add a pious or 'theological' note to teaching which was originally given on the sole authority of a human teacher. Each instruction has its own character as an independent piece. In the three cases mentioned above, it is true that a redactor has thought it necessary to insert a reminder that, despite the apparently absolute claims by the teacher for the effectiveness of his teaching provided that it is heeded, his authority is in fact subject to that of Yahweh and that ultimately it is Yahweh who is in control of human lives. This does not, however, necessarily mean that the original instructions are to be regarded as 'secular' or as setting up a human authority above that of God. The Yahweh additions where they occur bring to the original instructions no more than a reminder of what both author and reader already know. There is no reason to suppose that the pupil was unaware or heedless of the claims of Yahweh on him,[20] although the high social status which appears to have been that of the pupils may have made such a reminder particularly necessary.

A Comparison of the Original Instructions

Although there are close similarities between the instructions, particularly as regards the introductions, there are notable differences between them not only in the themes dealt with but also in style. These differences suggest multiple authorship though within a fairly closely-knit circle of like-minded instructors and pupils or readers.

Proverbs 1.8-19

Here, where the theme is the fate which awaits those who participate in group violence and crime, there is a vivid picture of a hypothetical situation couched in a conditional sentence, which includes direct speech—the words of the gang of youths (vv. 11-14)—followed by an admonition (v. 15) with motive clauses (vv. 16-18) and concluding with a general statement about the fate of those who indulge in violence.

Proverbs 2.1-22

The style of this instruction is quite different. Instead of the series of imperatives with which the father begins in 1.8-19 (and the other instructions), virtually the whole instruction takes the form of a conditional sentence. The theme is that of the dangers posed by the plausible adulteress, from whom the father's teaching is able to save the young man. The general statement with which the instruction ends, however, is, if original or partly so, comparable with the concluding verses of 1.8-19 This instruction is isolated from the other instructions on the same theme by the interpolation of a series of instructions on other themes.

---

20. I do not agree with McKane's view (*Proverbs*, p. 8) that while most of the instructions 'inculcate earthly and hard-headed wisdom and have nothing in them that would stamp them as distinctively Israelite, certainly not as Yahwistic', in those 'few places' where 'the Instruction has been brought into the field of Yahwistic piety' it 'retains no recognizable contact with its primary educational *Sitz*'.

Proverbs 3.1-12
This instruction also has its own character. It is the only instruction which is concerned with duties towards Yahweh; and although it has a single theme, its main body takes the form of three (four) separate admonitions with motive clauses each promising a good result from paying attention to the teaching. It is separated from the following instruction by a wisdom poem or poems (vv. 13-20).

Proverbs 3.21-35
The introduction to this instruction includes the unique feature of a reference to the various occasions during the course of the day when the teacher's words will protect the pupil: when he is walking, sitting (reading *tēšēb*, on the basis of LXX, in place of MT's *tiškab*, which is repetitive) and lying down to sleep (vv. 23-24). These verses (22-24) are reminiscent of Deut. 6.6-9 and 11.18-20, where it is the authoritative words of the Law that are to be kept in mind on such occasions. This feature does not occur in any of the other introductions. In the main body of the instruction, which is concerned with relations with neighbours, there is a certain similarity with 3.1-12 on duties towards Yahweh, in that it consists not of a single admonition but of a number of admonitions on the same general theme, in this case five (vv. 27-31). Another similarity with 3.1-12 is that this instruction originally had no general conclusion but ended quite abruptly.

Proverbs 4.1-9
As has already been noted, this instruction may be incomplete. As it stands, its main body is quite unlike any of the other instructions in several respects: it is couched in the form of a narrative; it has the character of a personal reminiscence; the only instruction given is in the form of reported speech and has no real content, as the teacher's father as quoted does no more than to repeat the contents of the introduction (v. 5bc). Even in its present augmented form this instruction contains no concrete, specific instruction whatever. The fact that it is addressed to 'sons' rather than to 'my son' also distinguishes it from all the other instructions. It is conceivable that it originally stood at the beginning of a longer instruction or group of instructions with the purpose of making it clear that the teacher had not invented his own material, that his authority was not personal to himself; that the

teaching to be given had the authority of antiquity and tradition, having been passed down from one generation to the next. But there is nothing in the text to give direct support to this speculation.

Proverbs 4.10-19

The theme of this instruction is the same as that of 1.8-19 and is expressed in a similar manner except for the absence of direct speech, which makes it less vivid. The admonition 'Do not enter the path of the wicked, and do not walk in the way of evildoers' (v. 14) is particularly close to 1.15: 'My son, do not walk in their way; keep your feet from their paths'.

Proverbs 4.20-27

The main body of this instruction (vv. 23-27) resembles 3.27-32 in that it consists of a series of admonitions (five) with a common general theme. It could be seen as making a deliberate contrast with 4.10-19 in that it is concerned with the inward disposition rather than with overt action. The admonitions are linked by their references to a series of bodily organs which represent different aspects of moral character: heart, mouth/lips, eyes, feet. Like 3.1-12 and 3.21-35 the instruction ends abruptly.

Proverbs 5.1-23; 6.20-35; 7.1-27

The similarities between all these instructions and also between each of them and 2.1-22 are so striking that some kind of direct connection between them may be regarded as probable. (It is theoretically possible that they are all independent examples of a fixed educational tradition; but it is more probable that imitation has taken place.) However, it is not possible to determine which was the model for others, or exactly how the plagiarism proceeded. But the very similarity of the four instructions speaks against any possibility that the ten instructions in these chapters once constituted a single teacher's manual or students' textbook. Whatever may have been the cause of their all being collected together, it was not that.

The following are the main similarities between the bodies of these four instructions (including 2.1-22):

1. With the exception of the instruction beginning in 5.1, from which a comparable verse appears to have been accidentally

omitted, the main section of each begins with a couplet in synonymous parallelism of which the first line reads 'to save/keep you from the *'iššâ zārâ* (literally, 'alien woman')/ *'ēšet rā'* ('woman of evil') and the second speaks of the *nokriyyâ* (also, literally, 'strange, alien woman') and her smooth speech (so 2.16; 6.24; 7.5). (5.3, although this couplet is lacking, also speaks of the *zārâ* whose speech is smoother than oil.)

2. Three of the instructions warn the pupil specifically to avoid the woman, again in couplets employing synonymous parallelism (5.8; 6.25; 7.25). In 2.16-19 this warning is implied.

3. All four give the same reason for avoiding association with the adulteress; three of them employ synonymous parallelism here also, stating in very similar words that if the young man goes with her she will lead him down to death and Sheol or 'the shades' (2.18; 5.5; 7.27; cf. perhaps 6.32, which is a general warning that the adulterer will 'destroy himself').

The Wisdom Poems

These three poems (1.20-33; 3.13-20; 8.1-36), the first two of which interrupt the sequence of the instructions, were originally independent poems. Although Scott surmised that 1.20-33 and ch. 8 were probably written by 'the author of the discourses' (i.e. the instructions), they differ too widely from them both in form and substance for this to be so, except perhaps for 3.13-18, which consists almost entirely of terminology and themes also found in the wisdom additions to the instructions: compare, for example, the stress on the importance of possessing and holding on to wisdom (3.13, 18) with 4.5, 7; the comparison of Wisdom's value with that of gold, silver and jewels (3.14-15) with 2.4; her gift of life and longevity (3.16, 18) with 3.22 and 4.13.

The portrayal of Wisdom in 1.20-33 and ch. 8 is not the same as in the instructions. She is no longer spoken of in the third person, but is herself a speaker: apart from the short introductions which set the scene (1.20-21; 8.1-3), the whole of these two long poems consists of her words, which she delivers in public. Instead of being a shadowy if important figure, she now appears as a fully fledged character.

Lang[21] regards 1.20ff. and ch. 8 as classroom teaching—a classification which he also applies to the instructions. It is not clear how he envisages their practical use in a class of children.[22] Bauer-Kayatz[23] had already pointed out the difficulty of such a position: even if, as Lang suggested is the case with 1.22-28, Wisdom's words could be interpreted as those of an exasperated teacher with a class of unwilling pupils, the words attributed to her in these two poems could not be used by a human being. There is a great difference between the pleas of the human teacher for attention in the instructions and the quasi-divine claims of Wisdom in these two speeches. In other words, although such claims were made *on behalf of* Wisdom in some of the instructions in their final form, nothing in the instructions could be said to have prepared the reader for Wisdom's own speeches.

In discussing these poems I am concerned with their literary unity and their functions in their present contexts rather than with the origins of the figure of Wisdom which they portray.

Proverbs 3.13-20

These verses, which are now placed between two instructions, were not composed as a single literary unit. Prov. 3.13-18, as has been recognized by a number of scholars, is a distinct composition complete in itself. After declaring 'happy the man who obtains Wisdom', it proceeds to list Wisdom's qualities and gifts somewhat in the style of a hymn, partly in figurative language (e.g. 'She is more precious than jewels', v. 15; 'She is a tree of life', v. 18) but mainly as a person ('her right hand', 'her left hand', v. 16; 'her ways', v. 17). That this is an originally independent poem is shown by the very obvious inclusio or bracketing device which binds the whole together: the initial word *'aš̆rê*, 'Happy (is)...' in v. 13 is echoed by

---

21. *Frau Weisheit: Deutung einer biblischen Gestalt* (Düsseldorf: Patmos, 1975), pp. 18ff. and *passim*.

22. Unless he means no more than that the author of the poem uses the language of the schoolroom and applies it to Wisdom (but he *seems* to mean more than this), he may mean that the whole poem, including the introductory vv. 20-21, is a school lesson spoken by the human teacher, in which he *quotes* Wisdom's speech; but he does not make this clear.

23. *Einführung in die alttestamentliche Weisheit* (Biblische Studien, 55; Neukirchen–Vluyn: Neukirchener Verlag, 1969), p. 64.

the final word in v. 18: the cognate $m^e\check{}u\check{s}\check{s}\bar{a}r$, '(made) happy', so making a complete statement.

Although much of what is said here is identical with statements made about Wisdom in some of the instructions, and the underlying purpose is the same—to encourage and persuade readers to devote themselves to the study of wisdom—the style is quite different. These verses are not simply an appendix to the previous instruction similar to, for example, 2.2-4, which does not constitute a complete independent sentence but is syntactically subordinate to what precedes.

Verses 19-20 are formally and thematically quite different again, both from vv. 13-18 and from the surrounding instructions. Wisdom is still a key feature of these verses, but is now seen as totally subordinate to Yahweh, who is the emphatic subject of the sentence. (In vv. 13-18 Wisdom is the only 'person' mentioned, and is spoken of as if she were the sole source of human wellbeing in the world.) This is a statement about Yahweh's action in the past (the verbs are in the perfect tense): it is an affirmation that it is he who founded the earth and the heavens, but that he did this *by wisdom* ($b^e\d{h}okm\hat{a}$). It is a very brief statement, and it is not clear why in v. 20 one particular feature of this creative activity is singled out. These two verses may be only a fragment of an originally longer poem (cf. 8.22-29; Isa. 40.12-14).

That vv. 19-20, though originally (part of?) a wholly independent poem, have been deliberately appended to vv. 13-18 seems clear. The purpose was somewhat similar to that which occasioned the addition of 2.5-9 to 2.2-4: to make it clear that the wisdom whose possession is so desirable is Yahweh's own wisdom. But the passage to which vv. 13-20, taken together, are most closely related is found within these same chapters: namely, ch. 8. Scott indeed goes so far as to say that 3.13-20 'look like an earlier draft of chapter viii'.[24] Apart from the difference in their length, there is of course one great difference between the two passages: 3.13-20 refers to Wisdom in the third person, while in ch. 8 it is Wisdom herself who is the speaker, talking about herself. Nevertheless, both passages, seen as a whole, consist of praise of Wisdom, her character and her gifts, while incorporating a briefer statement that she was closely associated with Yahweh when he created the world.

24. *Proverbs/Ecclesiastes*, p. 16.

As has already been suggested, the present position of 3.13-18 may be due to an editorial decision to introduce Wisdom into a context (i.e., the preceding instruction, 3.1-12) in which she had not been mentioned (apart from the line 'Do not be wise in your own eyes' in v. 7a). Furthermore, it may be that some affinity with 3.1-12 was perceived by this editor which made these verses an appropriate addition: the claim in v. 16 that Wisdom confers long life and wealth on her possessors may be seen as a comment on v. 2, where long life is stated to be the consequence of heeding the father's teaching, and v. 10, where wealth is promised to those who honour Yahweh. When vv. 13-18 were placed here, vv. 19-20 were probably already attached to them.

Proverbs 1.20-33[25]

Despite the facts that both 1.20-33 and 8.1-36 consist of speeches made in public by a personified Wisdom (which makes them unique in the Old Testament), that each speech is preceded by a very similar introduction describing a similar setting (1.20-22; 8.1-3), and that the audience is the same in each case—the 'simple ones' ($p^e t \bar{a} yim$, 1.22; $p^e t \bar{a}' yim$, 8.5)—the two are very different. They do, however, both belong to the same basic tradition as the wisdom additions to the instructions and as 3.13-18, the tradition of a personified Wisdom who can confer great gifts on those who seek her; and, with regard to the history of this tradition, which is not found anywhere else in the Hebrew Bible, it is pertinent to enquire which represents the earlier and which the later development: whether 1.20-33 and 8.1-36 are later, more highly developed examples of the tradition than the passages in the instructions, or whether the latter are summary forms of a longer tradition, cut down to make them suitable for a new function.

In 1.20-33 Wisdom does not speak in great detail about her gifts. In vv. 22-24 she addresses the 'simple' and the fool in the role of teacher, urging them to pay attention to her words; but in vv. 24-25 she accuses them of having already rejected her call and her teaching; and in vv. 26-27 she disdains all further responsibility for their

25. See, apart from Lang, *Wisdom and the Book of Proverbs*, pp. 19-50, the discussion of this poem by M. Gilbert, 'Le discours menaçant de sagesse en Proverbes 1.20-33', in *Storia e tradizioni di Israele: Scritti in onore di J. Alberto Soggin* (Brescia: Paideia, 1991), pp. 99-119.

welfare, saying that she will laugh at their misfortune when it comes. Then in v. 28 there comes a change. Wisdom now drops her second-person address to the simple and begins to speak in similar terms *about* persons who will call to her and seek her: she will not answer their call for help, and they will not find her; they will get the fate that they deserve (vv. 29-31). These persons are referred to in the *third* person. The poem concludes with a general statement in which Wisdom contrasts the fates of the simple and the fools with the security which will be enjoyed by those who listen to her (vv. 32-33).

The change from second-person address to third-person reference in v. 28 creates a problem which commentators have attempted to elucidate in various ways but without success. It cannot be dismissed as inadvertent, since it persists through several verses, and the chapter never returns to the second-person address; and it seriously weakens the dramatic effect of Wisdom's speech. The most probable solution— in opposition to the general scholarly consensus that the whole of 1.20-33 is a literary unity—may be that vv. 28-31 are a somewhat clumsy interpolation into the original speech comparable with additions which have been made to some of the instructions (especially in chs. 5 and 6) which also are singled out by changes of style and reference. The general statements in vv. 32-33, however, are probably original: they correspond to similar verses concluding speeches by the teachers in some of the instructions, they revert to the personal pronoun ('those who listen to me') in the final verse, and they round off the entire speech by repeating Wisdom's plea for attention made at the beginning (v. 23).

It is of particular interest to note that it is in the interpolated verses that the only reference to Yahweh occurs (v. 29b). This verse identifies 'knowledge' (*da'at*), which in these chapters is frequently synonymous with wisdom, with the 'fear of Yahweh' (cf. 1.7). If we set aside as unduly speculative Lang's view that this verse originally spoke of 'the fear of the gods' but was subsequently altered to its present Yahwistic form, it may be seen as an interpolation made for the same reason as the Yahweh additions in some of the instructions: to make it clear that to choose Wisdom is synonymous with choosing obedience to Yahweh. The verse stands out as an anomaly in a poem entirely concerned with the figure of wisdom, which gives dramatic expression to the idea that the acceptance or rejection of Wisdom and her counsel is the sole cause of human fortune or misfortune. It appears to be an interpolation within an interpolation. From both a literary and a thematic point of view it is a redundancy: vv. 30-31, which attribute the disaster which will follow to those who reject Wisdom, say all that needs to be said.

From a theological point of view, however, v. 29 has a point to make. It has been observed[26] that both speeches by Wisdom (1.20-33 and ch. 8) immediately follow instructions. In the case of 1.20-33, the instruction which precedes (1.8-19) is one which mentions neither Wisdom nor Yahweh; it may therefore be reasonably supposed that 1.20-33, although it had originally had an independent existence, was placed in its present position for the same reason that comparable additions were made to certain of the instructions: to interpret the teaching given by the father in that instruction in terms both of Wisdom and of the fear of Yahweh.

Proverbs 8.1-36[27]

Like 1.20-33 this poem, after a short introduction which sets the scene (vv. 1-3), consists wholly of a speech by personified Wisdom. The tone, however, is quite different from that of 1.20-33. Whereas in ch. 1 Wisdom has almost nothing positive or encouraging to say, but is mainly concerned to denounce those who refuse to heed her advice in such strong terms as to give the impression of having been motivated by some unsatisfactory experience (though not necessarily that of a rebellious classroom, *pace* Lang!), ch. 8 is almost entirely positive, dwelling on the good things that are attainable by those who become Wisdom's disciples.

The chapter falls into five sections: vv. 1-3, 4-11, 12-21, 22-31, 32-36. Verses 1-3 set the scene: Wisdom makes a public speech. This begins in v. 4 with an address not only to the simple and foolish but to humankind in general: the 'sons of man'. In vv. 5-6, however, Wisdom does appeal especially to the simple and foolish, urging them to acquire the intellectual qualities which they lack by heeding her words. In vv. 6-9 she claims that her teaching is of the highest morality, and in vv. 10-11 she speaks in conventional terms of its

---

26. E.g. by Meinhold, *Die Sprüche*, p. 44.

27. See further M. Gilbert, 'Le discours de la sagesse en Proverbes, 8. Structure et cohérence', in M. Gilbert (ed.), *La sagesse de l'Ancien Testament* (BETL, 51; Gembloux: Duculot; Leuven: Leuven University Press, 1979), pp. 202-18.

great value, although v. 11, which speaks of her in the third person and is virtually identical with 3.15, is probably a gloss.

In the third section, which is prefaced by the introductory formula 'I, Wisdom', she enlarges further on her virtues and power, asserting *inter alia* that it is through her that kings reign (vv. 15-16), that she loves those who love her (the 'bride' motif again, v. 17) and that she will bestow on them wealth and prosperity (vv. 18-21).

The fourth section (vv. 22-31) is quite different in character, and is generally regarded by the commentators as an originally independent poem, although in its present form taken by itself it lacks an introductory formula identifying Wisdom as the speaker. It is widely regarded as partly dependent on mythological themes. Kayatz, who detects Egyptian influence throughout the chapter in contrast with 1.20-33, compares this text with Egyptian texts which speak of the goddess Maat and her relation to Atum, while Lang thinks of an Israelite goddess of wisdom. However this may be, the most important fact about these verses from the point of view of the composition of the chapter as a whole is their introduction of Yahweh together with their assertion of Wisdom's total dependence on him. They constitute, apart from two brief allusions in vv. 13 and 35, the only reference in the chapter to him. Otherwise it is Wisdom, the speaker in a poem of self-praise, who is its dominant and indeed sole personality, making absolute claims for herself. Here, on the contrary, it is Yahweh who is the subject: it is he who created the world, with Wisdom in a subordinate position. This is an explicitly Yahwistic passage. Wisdom still makes claims for herself, but her very claim of closeness to Yahweh betrays her inferiority and so implicitly confesses that all good things do *not*, except perhaps indirectly, come from her. There is thus an implied contradiction between these verses and the rest of the chapter.

As has been suggested above, there is a strong similarity between Wisdom's speech in this chapter (including vv. 22-31) and 3.13-20. Although in the latter passage Wisdom is only referred to in the third person, and although there is no clear personification of her in vv. 19-20 (the statement that Yahweh founded the earth by wisdom, $b^e hokm\hat{a}$, with no further elaboration, would most naturally be interpreted as saying no more than that Yahweh, being wise, used his intelligence in performing this action), both passages have similar contents and are expressed in similar terms. Both urge the acquisition of wisdom and present it as incomparably valuable (3.14-15; 8.10-11) and as able to confer riches and honour (3.16; 8.18; 21), and both then abruptly introduce statements about the creation of the world by Yahweh in which Wisdom is somehow involved.

It is clear that in both cases the statement about Yahweh has been superimposed on a passage that was originally concerned only with Wisdom. From the point of view of the composition of these chapters it must be asked which of the two poems has the priority. This question is not easy to answer, especially as it is possible that 3.19-20 may be only a fragment of a longer poem (see above). It is possible that 3.13-20 is dependent on ch. 8 but in a deliberately abbreviated form; but it is perhaps more probable that 3.13-18, with its third-person presentation of Wisdom, occupies an intermediate position between passages like 2.2-4 and 4.5-9, which are somewhat similar in content but not independent poems, and ch. 8, in which Wisdom has developed into a fully fledged female figure speaking in the first person in praise of herself.

The final section of the chapter (vv. 32-36) resumes the original speech by Wisdom that was interrupted in v. 21. It rounds off the speech with a further appeal to pay attention to Wisdom's teaching, concluding by presenting the audience with a choice between 'life' for those who find her and injury for those who fail to do so. The text of these verses, however, is in disorder, and additions have been made to it.[28] The original text may be reconstructed as follows:

34a	Happy is the man who listens to me,
32b	and happy are those who keep my ways,
34b	watching daily at my gates
34c	waiting beside my doors.
35a	For he who finds me finds life,
36a	but he who misses me injures himself.

Verse 32a is an obvious intrusion, presumably made in order to make a smooth transition between vv. 22-31 and the interrupted conclusion of Wisdom's speech by inserting a resumptive formula. But the line is quite unsuited to its context: 'my children' as a form of address is nowhere else used by Wisdom; rather, it is (mainly in the singular, but cf. 4.1) the formula with which the human teacher begins his instructions. This line is verbally identical with 7.24a, whence it has been inappropriately imported.

28. See Whybray, 'Some Literary Problems', pp. 492-96 for a fuller discussion.

Verse 35b, which interrupts the antithetical parallelism between vv. 35a and 36a, is a rather trite addition which is also found in 18.22b. Like v. 13a, which is another subsequent addition made to Wisdom's original speech, conspicuous because it creates a three-line verse, it is intended to serve a similar purpose to vv. 22-31, making clear the close relationship which exists between Wisdom and Yahweh: the 'life' offered by Wisdom in v. 35a is identified with Yahweh's favour.

Like 1.20-33, ch. 8 immediately follows an instruction: 7.1-27, the final instruction in the series. Unlike 1.8-19 this is not an instruction to which no references to wisdom have been added: Wisdom is briefly mentioned as a prospective 'bride' in 7.4. (There are, however, no references to Yahweh in ch. 7.) On the other hand, the juxtaposition of ch. 8 with ch. 7 has a particular appropriateness in that the female figure of Wisdom in ch. 8 can readily be interpreted as a counterpart to an antithesis of the women portrayed in the instruction, particularly in the final form of the latter. There are many verbal as well as topical links between the two passages. Both Wisdom and the adulteress stand in the public places of the town (8.1-3; 7.12) and call to the simple (8.5; 7.7), and their persuasive words are quoted (8.4-10, 32-36; 7.14-20). Both offer 'love' (8.17; 7.18); both mention the house as a rendezvous (8.34; 7.8, 27); while Wisdom speaks of her 'ways' as righteous and just (8.20), the teacher warns the pupil against straying into the woman's 'ways'. Finally, Wisdom offers 'life' (8.35a), while the adulteress's house 'goes down to the chambers of death' (7.27). Chapter 8 in its final form also introduces the theme of Yahweh as closely associated with Wisdom, a feature lacking in ch. 7.

Proverbs 9

There is widespread agreement among the commentators that this chapter comes from a somewhat different tradition from that represented by chs. 1–8, although, if that is so, the two traditions cannot be very different. In the first part of the chapter, vv. 1-6, Wisdom is personified, and, as in 1.20-33 and ch. 8, issues a public invitation to the simple and fools, this time from the 'high places of the town' ($m^e r\bar{o}m\hat{e}\ q\bar{a}ret$; cf. 8.2, where the same word $m^e r\hat{o}m\hat{i}m$ is used), to her house to accept what she has to offer. (There is an obvious link here with ch. 8 in the statement in v. 1 that she has built her house: 8.34bc refers to its gates and doors, 9.1 to its pillars.)

In fact it is probable that these verses do not come from a different tradition but are based on what has been said in the earlier chapters about Wisdom and about her antithesis, the adulteress. The style is different from both that of the instructions and that of the other wisdom poems, and so is the imagery; the latter, however, is partly based on the narrative in 7.6-23 about the adulteress, for what Wisdom offers here is not advice but a *meal* at her house (compare 7.14, where this is the initial excuse for the adulteress's invitation). Meinhold[29] suggests that these verses, together with vv. 13-18, are intended to form the conclusion to chs. 1–9 and to give an explanation of their symbolism—in other words, to make explicit what is only implicit there. Certainly their intention was to bring the earlier teaching to a climax and to leave readers with a vivid and unforgettable impression of the choice which they have to make between 'life' and 'death'.

But vv. 1-6 by themselves are insufficient to create this vivid impression: vv. 13-18 are needed to complete it. Although some commentators (e.g. Scott, Goldingay[30]) consider vv. 13-18 to be a later addition, it is not easy to understand the grounds for such a view. Verses 1-6 and 13-18 are to be understood as a 'diptych', in which each leaf mirrors, yet contrasts with, the other. The two passages parallel one another closely but with all-important differences. The subject of vv. 13-18 is 'the woman Folly' (*'ēšet kᵉsîlût*), a figure who does not appear elsewhere, but who has replaced the adulteress as the antithesis of Wisdom. Features of the adulteress, however, remain: what the woman Folly offers to the young man is 'stolen water' and 'secret food', that is, clearly, illicit sexual relations whose acceptance will, as with the adulteress, lead to death (v. 18; cf. 2.18-19; 5.5; 7.27). Nevertheless she is the antithesis of Wisdom: she is not only foolish but also entirely ignorant (*bal-yādᵉ'â mâ*, v. 13): that is, she represents that lack of knowledge (*da'at*) which the teacher of the instructions regards as essential. Like Wisdom, she has her own house, but unlike Wisdom she calls to the young men from her doorway, not from the public places of the town. The first part of her speech

---

29. Meinhold, *Die Sprüche*, p. 151

30. J.E. Goldingay, 'Proverbs V and IX', *RB* 84 (1977), pp. 87-93, offers an alternative view of the composition of this chapter.

(v. 16) is exactly the same as that of Wisdom (v. 4), but what she has to offer (v. 17) is the antithesis of the wholesome food offered by Wisdom (v. 5). Whereas Wisdom offers life (v. 6) she is offering death (v. 18), but the simple do not know this.

These two passages considered together make an effective contrast and constitute an impressive literary unity. It is, of course, theoretically possible that 9.13-18 was subsequently modelled on 9.1-6 and then appended to it, but there is no evidence that this was the case. One of the chief features of the preceding chapters is their predilection for contrasts, especially their constant portrayal of the 'two ways' leading respectively to life and death, between which a choice must be made, and it is natural that the final chapter of this section of the book should also use this pedagogic device. It is also perhaps significant that the only other reference to Wisdom's house in the book (14.1a) is immediately followed (14.1b) by a reference to the destructive activity of 'folly'.

Verses 7-12, which separate the two vignettes of Wisdom and Folly, have been treated very differently by scholars. A common view has been that their presence here is due to a misunderstanding or to a scribal error:[31] they interrupt the sequence of vv. 1-6 and 13-18 and are irrelevant to it. On the other hand, some scholars have taken a more positive view of these verses, maintaining, for example, that they play an important role in the structure not only of chs. 1–9 but of the whole book of Proverbs.[32]

The text of these verses must be admitted to be unstable; and this instability may extend to the final part of the chapter as well. LXX has a longer text: it has three additional couplets after v. 12 and a further three after v. 18. Such additional material in the LXX of Proverbs is not unusual, and does not necessarily indicate a lacuna in MT; more significant, however, is the fact that *BHS* records that vv. 9-10 are entirely missing from one Hebrew manuscript, and that vv. 10-12 are entirely missing from another.

That vv. 7-12 do not constitute a single literary unit is clear: their

---

31. So, e.g., B. Gemser, *Sprüche Salomos* (HAT, 16; Tübingen: Mohr, 2nd edn, 1963), p. 51; H. Ringgren, *Sprüche Salomos* (ATD, 16; Göttingen: Vandenhoeck & Ruprecht, 2nd edn, 1967 [1962]), p. 42; Lang, *Frau Weisheit*, p. 19; *idem*, *Wisdom and the Book of Proverbs*, p. 87.

32. So especially Meinhold, *Die Sprüche*, p. 150.

contents are miscellaneous. Some of the material pertains to the nature of instruction: vv. 8, 9, 11 and 12 are all addressed to a single person, vv. 8 and 9 being couched in the singular imperative as though expressing a teacher's demands to a pupil. It would be natural to suppose that the teacher in question is the speaker of vv. 4-6, that is, Wisdom herself, although some of the material is unlike anything that Wisdom says elsewhere. Verse 7, for example, is an impersonal statement of a formal type frequently found in chs. 10–29. There is only one of these verses in which the identity of the speaker is clearly indicated: that is v. 11, where it may be assumed that it is Wisdom herself who says, 'For by me (*bî*) your days will be multiplied'.

A brief account of each of these verses will indicate their character. Verse 7, as already stated, is a general statement similar in form to many in chs. 10–29. It is an isolated proverb. Verse 8 has a similar subject and uses some of the same vocabulary (*lēṣ*, 'scoffer', *hôkîaḥ*, 'rebuke'), but is a (double) admonition addressed to a single person; there is no reason to suppose that these two verses were originally connected. Verse 9 is similar to 1.5. Verse 10 stands out clearly from its context: not only is this the only reference to Yahweh in the chapter but it is also an impersonal and quite general maxim or motto concerning the nature of wisdom, to which it refers in the third person and without any suggestion of personification, asserting its close relationship or near-identity with 'the fear of Yahweh'. Its first line is virtually identical with 1.7a, with only slight differences of vocabulary. Verse 11, which begins with *kî* ('For'), purports to enlarge upon the statements of v. 10 by promising longevity to those who take them to heart; but this is a personal statement by a personified Wisdom, making for herself the kind of claims that she makes in her other speeches. The purpose of the final verse of the section, v. 12, is unclear. It consists of two parallel conditional sentences addressed to a single person in the manner of a teacher, and appears to limit the effects both of wisdom and of 'scoffing' respectively to the person who possesses or practices them. This notion, which seems to contradict the usual teaching of these chapters that wisdom can be communicated to others as also can wickedness, has nothing in common with the preceding verses and is an isolated comment.

It is hardly possible to dismiss the whole of these verses as totally irrelevant to their immediate context, though at the same time the relevance of some of them remains obscure. Much scholarly ingenuity

has been expended in attempts to account for the presence of this
material in its present position, to explain the relationships of these
verses to one another, and to show that they have wider contextual
relationships connected with the redaction of the book of Proverbs as
a whole.

One certain fact is that there are connections between some of these
verses and ch. 1, or at least with 1.1-7. The resemblance between
v. 10 and 1.7 is undeniable; and v. 9 also echoes 1.5, even to the
repetition of a particular phrase, $w^e y \hat{o} s e p \ l e q a h$, 'and he will gain in
learning'. The former has led some scholars[33] to postulate that v. 10,
perhaps together with vv. 11-12, originally concluded the chapter,
forming, together with 1.7, a thematic framework to chs. 1–9. This
would mean either that vv. 13-18 were added subsequently (on this
view see above), or that vv. 7-12 (or part of them) have been
accidentally misplaced, having originally followed vv. 13-18. Lang[34]
saw vv. 7-10 as a final warning to undisciplined students.

Preuss and Meinhold[35] further understood these verses as having a
wider function: as serving as a transitional passage (*Zwischenstück*)
between chs. 1–9 and 10.1–22.16. While it is true that some of this
material (especially vv. 7, 8 and 12) has formal and thematic resemb-
lances to proverbs in 10.1–22.16. while also retaining characteristics
of the chapters which precede, 10.1–22.16 is a clearly defined
collection of proverbs with its own heading. It is difficult to see why
such a transition between these two quite different types of wisdom
literature should have been thought necessary, how it would have
functioned and why it should have been effective. While it is generally
and correctly recognized that chs. 1–9 in their final form were
intended to serve as a 'preface' to the rest of the book, the clear
indications in the text of the extent of the book's various constitutive
parts will have been sufficient guides to the material as a whole, and
much more effective than a gradual, 'transitional' style would have
been. The key to the relationship between chs. 1–9 and 10.1–22.16 is
not to be found in these verses.

The problems of 9.7-12 have not been satisfactorily solved, and any
conclusions reached must be very tentative. It is not necessary here to

33. Scott, *Proverbs/Ecclesiastes*, p. 16; Lang, *Frau Weisheit*, p. 88.
34. *Wisdom and the Book of Proverbs*.
35. Preuss, *Einführung*, p. 60; Meinhold, *Die Sprüche*, p. 45.

record all the permutations of theories about the originality or connections of this or that verse.

The obvious affinity between 9.10 and 1.7 suggests that those two verses have been deliberately placed in their present positions in order to enclose the whole of chs. 1–9, with the exception of the general introduction (1.1-6), within a general affirmation of the understanding of the meaning of Wisdom by the redactor who placed them there (we may compare the function of Eccl. 1.2 and 12.8 with regard to that book). On the other hand, there is no evidence in either text or versions that vv. 7-12 or 7-10 were transferred wholesale from the end of the chapter to their present position, and no other reason to suppose that vv. 13-18 are a subsequent addition to the chapter.

However, the misplacing of a single verse is quite a different matter from the misplacing of a longer passage. It is easily possible for a verse accidentally omitted in copying and subsequently replaced in the margin of a manuscript to be wrongly replaced in the text when a further copy is made—a not uncommon phenomenon in the history of the Hebrew text of the Old Testament. It is, then, a possibility—but only a possibility—that this occurred in the case of v. 10.

Verse 11, which is clearly intended to be seen as spoken by Wisdom, is probably not in fact a continuation of her words from vv. 4-6, which have their own perfectly satisfactory conclusion. It was probably composed in an attempt to create the impression that the verses between, which had already been inserted into the text, belong to Wisdom's speech.

The remaining material in vv. 7-12 can plausibly be explained as examples of the kind of debris—here concerned with various types of wisdom—which tended to collect at the end of some of the instructions, for example 3.32-35. It is couched mainly in the form of proverbs like those found in chs. 10.1–22.16—a fact which has led to the mistaken conclusion that these verses consciously 'look forward' to those later chapters—and which a redactor thought it appropriate to add here as germane to Wisdom's teaching.

Proverbs 6.1-19

It is generally agreed by the commentators that these verses lie outside the pattern of fathers' instructions and wisdom poems which characterizes chs. 1–9; and in particular that they interrupt the series of instructions about the danger posed by the adulteress which is otherwise the common theme of chs. 5–7. There is a sense in which they could be regarded as loosely appended to ch. 5, but the subjects with which they deal are quite distinctive, and the forms into which they are cast are uncharacteristic of these chapters; they have much greater affinities with other parts of the book of Proverbs.

Recent commentators, however, have pointed out that there are in fact links of various kinds with ch. 5 which may account for the present position of this additional material. The final verses of ch. 5, vv. 21-23, are observations of a general kind unconnected with the main theme of the chapter, about human behaviour (*dar*ᵉ*kê 'îš*, 'the ways of a man', v. 21), and in particular about the fates of the wicked (v. 22) and the foolish (v. 23). These are precisely the themes of 6.1-19: vv. 1-11 are concerned with particular forms of folly and their consequences, and vv. 12-19 similarly with the wicked and their fate. There are also some possible verbal links with ch. 5: Plöger[36] pointed out the use of the verb *lākad*, 'capture', 'ensnare' in 5.22 and 6.2 in references to disastrous consequences of human behaviour; Meinhold[37] and others have pointed to the use of *zār*, 'another (man)' in 6.1—that is, the masculine form of *zārâ*, the adulteress or 'wife of another' in ch. 5—which occurs not only in the earlier verses of that chapter but also in v. 20. This may have suggested the thought that just as one should avoid association with another man's wife, one should also be cautious in engaging in financial transactions with her husband! More generally, it may be relevant to point out that the instructions in chs. 1–9 are not confined to a discussion of sexual temptations with which a young man may be faced, and that 6.1-19 constitutes a reminder of this wider range of concerns.

Prov. 6.1-19 falls clearly into four sections: vv. 1-5, 6-11, 12-15 and 16-19. Each of these has the marks of an originally self-contained unit which is unrelated to the others both in contents and form except in so far as they are all concerned with types of human behaviour that are undesirable and dangerous.

Verses 1-5 bear a superficial resemblance to the instructions which may account for its initial position: it is addressed to 'my son', and

36. O. Plöger, *Sprüche Salomos (Proverbia)* (BKAT, 17; Neukirchen–Vluyn: Neukirchener Verlag, 1984), p. 62.
37. *Die Sprüche*, p. 108.

was probably instructional in the same way as some of the proverbs in chs. 10–29. But unlike the instructions in chs. 1–9 it entirely lacks an introductory section in which the father commends the importance of his teaching; it plunges straight into its matter: 'My son, if...' Its subject, the folly of pledging one's possessions as security for a neighbour, is not treated elsewhere in the instructions, but occurs relatively frequently among the proverbs of 10.1–22.16 and chs. 25–29: 11.15; 17.18; 20.16; 27.13. Here it is not restricted to a single couplet but is in an extended form comparable with other extended proverbs such as 27.23-27. Prov. 6.6-11 is an animal proverb—that is, it uses animal behaviour as a model to be imitated (cf. 30.24-32). It is a call to the lazy to stir themselves into activity. Its moral (vv. 10-11) is repeated in virtually the same words in another moral tale about the lazy, 24.33-34, a sign that it belongs to traditional popular wisdom.

Prov. 6.12-15, a description of a wicked man and the disaster which will fall upon him suddenly, in which his various activities are listed in terms of parts of the body (mouth, eyes, feet, fingers, heart) is also a piece of traditional wisdom. There is a similar device in vv. 17-18 and also in other passages in Proverbs.

Prov. 6.16-19 is a so-called 'numerical proverb' similar to those found in ch. 30, especially 30.18-19, 21-23, 29-31. It also has in common with vv. 12-15 the listing of parts of the body: eyes, tongue, hands, heart, feet; it also duplicates items listed there: $m^e šall\bar{e}a\d{h}$ $m^ed\bar{a}n\hat{\imath}m$, 'sowing dissension' (v. 19) parallels $m^ed\bar{a}n\hat{\imath}m$ $m^e šall\bar{e}a\d{h}$ i n v. 14b, and $l\bar{e}b$ $\d{h}\bar{o}r\bar{e}š$ $ma\d{h}š^eb\hat{o}t$ '$\bar{a}wen$, 'a heart that devises wicked plans' (v. 18) is synonymous with $b^elibb\hat{o}$ $\d{h}\bar{o}r\bar{e}š$ $r\bar{a}$ ' in v. 14a. Both these passages, then, describe the activities of a thoroughly evil person in somewhat similar terms; the main difference between them is that the activities mentioned in vv. 16-19 are stated to be things which are 'abomination to Yahweh'. This is the only reference to Yahweh in vv. 1-19. (Meinhold[38] pointed out that in ch. 5 also the sole reference to Yahweh occurs near the end [v. 21]; but it is doubtful whether this fact has any bearing on the question of the reasons why vv. 1-19 have been appended to ch. 5.)

To sum up, there is much to be said for the view that vv. 1-19 were intended as pertinent additions to the already rather overloaded and

38. *Die Sprüche*, p. 108.

diffuse ch. 5. With regard to possible internal connections *between* the four units, both Plöger and Meinhold[39] have argued that there is a progression or heightening of thematic gravity from each to the next, despite their obvious stylistic and formal diversity. This may be an overstatement; but it is true that these passages fall, at any rate, into two thematic groups: vv. 1-11 are concerned with folly and vv. 12-19 with wickedness. It could perhaps be said that a particular act of folly (vv. 1-5) is less serious than a persistent weakness of character (vv. 6-11); and although there appears to be no difference in the degrees of wickedness condemned in vv. 12-15 and 16-19, the claim in v. 16 that the things condemned in vv. 17-19 are particularly hateful to God may certainly be regarded as constituting a climax to the whole. These thematic relationships between the four pericopes are therefore probably to be seen as an indication that they had already been combined into a single unit before they were placed in their present position.

The Prologue: Proverbs 1.1-7

The first seven verses of the book of Proverbs are clearly of an introductory character. Whether they are to be regarded as introductory only to chs. 1–9 or to the whole book is a matter which has long been debated; there is in fact no reason why they should not have been intended to serve both purposes: a passage whose introductory function was originally restricted to those chapters may easily have been reapplied, perhaps with some modifications, to serve the larger work.

These verses are concerned with education in a broad sense: with learning, understanding, teaching.[40] The object of this education is

---

39. Plöger, *Sprüche Salomos*, pp. 65-66; Meinhold, *Die Sprüche*, p. 108.

40. The similarities between these verses and the preface to the Egyptian *Teaching of Amenemope* have often been noted, and a direct literary connection has sometimes been alleged. (There is an English translation of the *Amenemope* passage, 1.1-6, in *ANET*, p. 421.) There are undoubtedly similarities between the two passages, but also considerable differences. The Egyptian text has a specific social and professional background: it refers to the importance of good relationships with 'elders' and courtiers and to the carrying out of missions from which it is necessary to bring back accurate reports; the Proverbs passage has no comparable background and is much more general in character except for the allusion to the acquisition of a knowledge of types of wisdom discourse in v. 6, a feature which is lacking in

expressed in a bewildering array of synonyms and near-synonyms: *ḥokmâ*, 'wisdom', *mûsār*, 'instruction', *bînâ*, 'understanding', *haśkēl*, 'intelligence', *'ormâ*, 'shrewdness', *mᵉzimmâ*, 'prudence', *leqaḥ*, 'learning', *taḥbūlôt*, 'skill'; all these words except for *'ormâ* recur in the later parts of the book (i.e. from ch. 10 onwards), most of them frequently. The same is true of the verbs employed here: *yāda'*, 'to know', *hēbîn*, 'to understand', *lāqaḥ*, 'to acquire' (sc. instruction)', *šāma'*, 'to hear, pay attention', *qānâ*, 'to acquire', and *hôsîp leqaḥ*, 'to increase in learning'. The verses contain no direct reference to the 'father' or teacher of the instructions or to a 'son' (although no such reference is necessarily to be expected in a general introduction); but it is quite clear that vv. 1-7 in their present form would be entirely appropriate as an introduction to the whole book of Proverbs, which is above all a book of instruction.

There are, however, reasons to suppose that vv. 1-7 are not homogeneous: that material has been added to an original core. A variety of attempts has been made to reconstruct a supposedly original and shorter form. The most extreme of these is that of Renfroe.[41] On the basis of differences of length of the constituent poetical lines as measured by the number of consonants which they contain, together with supposed differences of theme and of intended readership, Renfroe has concluded not only that the introduction was originally considerably shorter than its final form, but also that the original arrangement of the lines has been quite severely disorganized. He holds that the original title of the passage was v. 6b, and that this was followed by vv. 4ab, 2ab, 3a and 6a. Verses 3b and 5 are later additions of considerable significance, v. 3b correcting the secular and non-ethical tone of the preceding lines and v. 5 broadening the spectrum of the audience. Verse 1 remains the general heading and v. 7, not dealt with by Renfroe, presumably does not belong to the passage.

Renfroe does not explain how or why the original order of the lines has been so ruthlessly disarranged, and his meticulous search for inconsistencies precluding single authorship may have been over-

---

Amenemope. Both passages stand within an international tradition, but a direct connection between them is improbable.

41. F. Renfroe, 'The Effect of Redaction on the Structure of Prov. 1.1-6', *ZAW* 101 (1989), pp. 290-93.

zealous. Nevertheless, there are some points at which a number of other scholars would agree with him.

The heading (v. 1) describes what follows as 'The proverbs of Solomon'. The Hebrew word here rendered by 'proverb' (*māšāl*) has a much wider meaning than the English word: it can be used not only of a short saying or axiom such as those found in Prov. 10.1–22.16 and chs. 25–29, but of a considerable variety of utterances, some of which are of considerable length. These include the oracles of Balaam (Num. 23.7 and several times in Num. 23–24), certain speeches of Job (Job 27.1; 29.1), a psalm (Ps. 78.2) and an allegory (Ezek. 17.2). The term is thus as appropriate as a designation of the instructions and other poems in Proverbs 1–9 as of the short one-verse proverbs of chs. 10–29, or indeed of any section of the book, although the words 'of Solomon' in this verse presumably exclude a reference to chs. 30–31, since those chapters are specifically attributed, under separate headings, to other people. This heading, then, offers no clue as to whether it originally referred only to chs. 1–9 (or part of them) or is an addition made at a relatively late stage embracing most of the book.

The heading, however, does not stand in isolation. Although it is in prose, it is integrally connected with the poetical lines which follow. Verses 2, 3, 4 and 6 are infinitive clauses ('for knowing', 'for acquiring', 'for giving', 'for understanding') whose function is to set out the purposes of the *mešālîm* in question; they cannot be independent sentences, but are syntactically dependent on v. 1. It therefore seems reasonable to suppose that vv. 1-4 and 6 belong to the same stratum, at whatever stage that may have been composed.

Some objections have been made to this judgment. Renfroe questioned the originality of v. 3b, which consists of a triad of ethical terms attached to the infinitive of v. 3a as additional objects, on the grounds that these are out of keeping with their context, and also detected a change of point of view in v. 4 from that of the pupil ('for learning', etc.) to that of the teacher or of the proverbs themselves ('for teaching'): the proverbs, from being the object of the verbs, have now become the subject. Renfroe found a solution to this second problem not by excising v. 4 but by transferring it to an earlier position in his rearranged text, where the change of point of view would be less harsh. This latter argument is probably hypercriticism: it would be unreasonable to expect such a high degree of logic in such a context as Renfroe appears to expect.

Renfroe's objection to the originality of v. 3b is more substantial; but the line is part of a poetical couplet, and would be difficult to omit unless, with Renfroe, one resorts to a wholesale rearrangement of all the lines. There is in fact no reason to suspect the originality of the line. These three ethical terms occur together also in 2.9, which has been seen above to be an original part of that instruction. The present study is not concerned to argue that ethical teaching was absent from the earlier stages of these chapters, and there is no reason to regard the line, as does Renfroe, as evidence of a 'social-ethical revolution which took place in the community which preserved this text in the period between its original composition and final redaction'.[42]

Plöger[43] regards vv. 5 and 6 as standing somewhat apart from vv. 2-4, although not, apparently, as a later addition. In his opinion the prologue as a whole has two purposes: to commend these *mᵉšālîm* to the young and uninstructed (vv. 2-4) and also to commend them to persons who already have some acquaintance with wisdom. The latter will be able to increase their knowledge and skill (v. 5) and, as 'experts', to attain to a more advanced knowledge of particular forms of wisdom literature so that they may be able to teach them to others. Plöger sees in v. 6 references to teaching at two levels; the specific forms listed there can be divided into two kinds: the young can be taught a *māšāl*, but the *mᵉlîṣâ* ('epigram'?) and the *ḥîdâ* ('riddle') belong to the higher education.

There can be no doubt that v. 5 is intended to broaden the scope of the prologue by affirming that these *mᵉšālîm* are as useful to those who are already wise as they are to beginners. A view alternative to that of Plöger is that the verse is an isolated interpolation or gloss (both Gemser and Plöger made this suggestion, although Plöger rejected this view in favour of that described above, and Gemser was not sure about it). Syntactically, it breaks the sequence of infinitive clauses which is the chief feature of vv. 2-4 and 6, being expressed in finite verbs in the jussive or imperfect, although if Plöger's view is right, the infinitive clauses in v. 6 are not a resumption of the series but are a new set attached to v. 5.

Whether v. 6 is understood as a continuation of v. 4 or of v. 5, it presents the advantages of the acquisition of wisdom in a way that is

---

42. Renfroe, 'The Effect of Redaction', p. 293.
43. *Sprüche Salomos*, pp. 9-10.

unique in the prologue, listing different types of wisdom literature. It stands apart somewhat from the preceding verses, which are very general in their commendation of wisdom. It is possible that v. 6 was added at the end of the prologue in order to extend its scope: if the preceding verses were written as a prologue to chs. 1–9, it may have been intended to embrace other kinds of proverb that are found in other parts of the book. *ḥîdâ* means a riddle (cf. Judg. 14; 1 Kgs 10.1), and examples of this type of proverb are probably to be found in Proverbs: one such may be 23.29, with the answer provided in v. 30; and there are other proverbs in the book which may originally have been in riddle form. The meaning of the rare word *mᵉlîṣâ*, which occurs only twice in the Old Testament, is uncertain; but it is probably another type of proverb, and it is at least possible that it is one which occurs in Proverbs 10–29 although it is not named there.

Some reference has already been made to v. 7. A few modern scholars have regarded vv. 7-9 as constituting a distinct unity;[44] but such a division of the text ignores or rejects the view expressed above that v. 8 is the beginning of a father's instruction, a view which now has a wide following. The view that, together with 9.10, 1.7 forms a framework embracing the whole of the teaching of chs. 1–9 and was added at a late stage in the formation of these chapters[45] appears to be most probable. If this is correct, it is in itself a kind of 'prologue'; but there is nothing to suggest that it was ever considered to be part of, or even an appendix to, vv. 1-6. It stands at the beginning of the *specific* instruction in these chapters; it negates neither what is said in vv. 1-6 nor the teaching of the first instruction (vv. 8-19) in which there is no reference to Yahweh; but, as the first reference to him in the book and in its identification of the 'wisdom' mentioned in v. 2 with the 'fear of Yahweh', it has been deliberately placed here to give the whole of these chapters a particular tone.

The process of the composition of 1.1-7 is, then, not easy to determine in detail; but the following may serve as a summary of what has been said above. It may be said with some confidence that from the first the prologue contained at least vv. 1-4; it was probably intended to form the prologue or introduction to the instructions in these

44. Gemser, *Sprüche Salomos*, pp. 19-20; Preuss, *Einführung*, p. 62.
45. Plöger, *Sprüche Salomos*; Meinhold, *Die Sprüche*; cf. Lang, *Wisdom and the Book of Proverbs*.

chapters at an early stage of their formation, since in it wisdom is still a common noun and Yahweh is not mentioned. Subsequently v. 5 was appended to the original core, with the intention of extending the commendation of the 'proverbs', originally intended only for young pupils, by asserting their usefulness even for those who were already 'wise'. Verse 6 was probably added when the prologue was adapted to cover other parts of the book. Finally, v. 7, which is an isolated verse unconnected with vv. 1-6 and forming a separate 'introduction' to the chapters which follow, was added together with 9.10 to form a framework to these chapters. This addition was probably made to mark out chs. 1–9 as a lengthy 'introduction' to the whole book.

The Composition of Chapters 1–9: Conclusions

The core of these chapters is to be found in the ten instructions in their original form. The rest of the material has been appended to them. They are educational in character and purpose, and there is no compelling reason to place their composition as late as the post-exilic period; nor is there a compelling reason to doubt that they are intended to represent the teaching of a real father given to his son, who may be presumed to be adolescent, still under his parents' tutelage but of an age to be subject to the temptations presented by both street gangs and immoral women. The situation is urban rather than rural, and the social status presupposed is high: wealth and worldly success are set before the pupil as a goal; wealth is presupposed (e.g. in 3.9-10); moreover, the kind of woman described in 7.6-23, whose house is filled with luxurious furnishings and goods, is unlikely to have set out to seduce a penniless and uncouth young man from outside her own social circle.

It is significant that poverty and the poor are never mentioned in these chapters. It is taken for granted that the reader shares the same social status as the writer, and no other interests than those belonging to that class fall under consideration.[46]

As has been suggested above, most of the instructions have been subject to expansions of various kinds; but two of them—1.8-19 and 4.20-27—are examples of a 'basic' model of parental instruction.

---

46. See R.N. Whybray, *Wealth and Poverty in the Book of Proverbs* (JSOTSup, 99; Sheffield: JSOT Press, 1990), pp. 99-106.

They consist simply of an introduction in which the father commends his own teaching, followed by a concrete admonition or admonitions; in one case at least some general remarks formed a conclusion. It was postulated that the remaining instructions originally conformed to that model. They were all of comparable length.

The ten instructions in their basic form combine close similarities with distinct differences. The introductory sections strongly resemble one another and to a large extent employ identical vocabulary, yet none is quite identical with another. The main sections differ considerably, yet four of them have an identical theme—the temptation of the adulteress—and to a large extent use identical language (e.g. 2.16; 6.24; 7.5). One (4.1-9) differs from all the others in that it consists of an 'instruction within an instruction', the father citing the teaching which had been given to him by his own father. It seems probable that the instructions belonged to a once more extensive genre from which an editor has made his own selection. It is possible that some of the similarities of language might be accounted for by imitation and assimilation undertaken in order to create an increased conformity; but if so the process has not been completely carried out; and the imitator has taken care *not* to use precisely the same words and phrases as his source.

The basis on which these particular instructions were chosen is not clearly apparent. They can hardly be said to constitute a compendium or educational 'syllabus', since they are manifestly both incomplete and repetitious. On the one hand, the short proverbs in the later part of the book offer a far greater range of topics that would have been suitable for the education of a young man; while on the other hand the inclusion of no less than four instructions on the temptations of the adulteress would seem to a modern reader to be grossly redundant. It is of course possible that whoever selected them was less concerned to construct a comprehensive course of instruction than to stress by repetition especially those particular temptations to which young men are vulnerable. In fact it is not only the original instructions that are concerned with this: and Aletti[47] perceptively notes that chs. 1–9 *as a whole* are primarily concerned with the theme of seduction. The young man is warned against the fatal attraction of a whole range of

47. J.-N Aletti, 'Séduction et parole en Proverbes I–IX', *VT* 27 (1977), pp. 129-44.

women; and as counter-attractions he is presented with the persuasive-ness of the father's teaching and of Wisdom, who offers herself as a bride as well as a teacher; and indeed with the attractions of a real down-to-earth human wife (5.15-19). How is the young man to be *persuaded* to set out on the right path, the one which will lead to life rather than death? This is, perhaps, the most important question that is asked here.

A further question is why the instructions are arranged in their present order. While it may be possible to point out some indications of a deliberate arrangement, it would be wrong to expect to find a completely logical and comprehensive one. On the other hand, Lang goes too far when he maintains that it is totally useless to expect to find any logical arrangement in any ancient wisdom text,[48] and that Proverbs 1–9 is no more than a haphazard, loose collection of unrelated material in which 'no text presupposes another'.[49]

It is true that indications of a deliberate arrangement of the instruc-tions are sparse. Several commentators have found significance in the fact that the (only) instruction concerned with behaviour towards God (3.1-12) is followed—after the interpolated 3.13-20—by an equally general one on behaviour towards one's neighbours (cf. the Decalogue). This sequence may, of course, be purely accidental, especially as it is not carried further. More likely to be deliberate, even though the reason for it is not clear to the modern reader, is the bunching together of three instructions on the same theme in chs. 5, 6 an 7 to form the conclusion of the series.

Otherwise it is difficult to see any thematic arrangement, especially since the second instruction (2.1-22), also concerning the adulteress, has been placed almost as far away as possible from the others which deal with the same subject. It should also be remembered that there is no proof that the ten instructions, or any of them, with or without a prologue, were ever assembled to form an independent work. Although they are almost certainly the earliest parts of chs. 1–9, they may have existed as separate instructions until they were combined with the other material now included in those chapters. There is in

---

48. B. Lang, *Die Weisheitliche Lehrrede: Eine Untersuchung von Sprüche 1–7* (SBS, 54; Stuttgart: KBW, 1972), p. 27.
49. Lang, *Frau Weisheit*, p. 18.

fact some evidence that this was so: they have not been treated in a consistent way by the augmenters.

Some of the additions which have been made to the original instructions are of a non-theological nature: they were made simply in order to put together material which had some similarity of theme: 5.9-23 is a good example of this (cf. also 6.1-19). There are no clues to the stage of composition at which material of this kind was added. The wisdom additions and Yahweh additions, however, represent attempts to *reinterpret* the instructions to which they were attached in specific ways. But the fact that some of the instructions have received no additions whatever, while others have been augmented by additions which equate the father's teaching with wisdom or with the fear of Yahweh, rules out any notion that there has been a *systematic* wisdom/Yahweh redaction. These additions have evidently been made to *individual* instructions.

The imagery of a personified Wisdom in some of the added material must be regarded as belonging to a more imaginative tradition than that which operates simply with the imagery of the authoritative father and his plain, down-to-earth teaching. As a teaching device it is likely to have been a subsequent development, of which the fully personified Wisdom who speaks and makes her own appeal in the wisdom poems clearly represents yet a further stage.

The Yahweh addition in 2.5-8 is appended to the wisdom addition of vv. 2-4, as is shown by its syntactical position, and must be seen as reinterpreting those verses. However, in other cases (3.26 and 5.21) the Yahweh material is quite independent of the wisdom material. As has already been observed, the paucity of references to Yahweh in the instructions, even in their augmented form, is remarkable: although one instruction is wholly concerned with behaviour towards Yahweh (3.1-12), elsewhere he does not play a major role. If there is no evidence of a systematic wisdom redaction of the instructions, there is certainly none of a systematic Yahweh redaction.

In their present position the three wisdom poems (3.13-20; 1.20-33; 8.1-36) appear to be appendices to the instructions which immediately precede them, fulfilling, though in their own way, a similar function to that of the 'theological' additions to them: that of introducing, or reinforcing, the point that the father's teaching is to be seen as related to, or as identical with, both wisdom and the fear of Yahweh. As originally independent poems, however, they have their own histories of composition. They belong to the tradition found in 2.2-4, 3.22, 4.5-7 and 4.13 in which Wisdom is personified, but carry it to a further stage of development. In the cases of 3.19-20 and 8.22-31, they then underwent a further development in which the wisdom which they portray was declared to be dependent on Yahweh (cf. the composition of 2.2-8).

It is impossible to determine the period either of the original composition of these poems or of this further development. The question turns mainly on whether such a highly sophisticated concept of wisdom could have been created before the Babylonian Exile; that is to say, it depends on the view taken of the history of the religion of Israel, about which there is at present great diversity of opinion. Many scholars are unwilling to pronounce on the matter. But Plöger and Meinhold are inclined to regard these poems, together with much else in chs. 1–9, as late, while, on the other hand, Kayatz and Lang see no reason, especially in view of supposedly comparable Egyptian literature, to rule out a pre-exilic date, though Lang sees ch. 8 as an early Israelite hymn to a pagan deity which was later—though still possibly before the Exile—altered to refer to Yahweh.

The twin vignettes of 9.1-6 and 13-18 portraying personified Wisdom and Folly are probably based upon the references to Wisdom and to the adulterous woman in the instructions, Wisdom's personification here being a development parallel to that of the wisdom poems and the personification of Folly being concomitant with it. They have been placed at the end of this part of the book in order to create a dramatic climax and to give an unforgettable lesson to the young man under instruction. The miscellaneous material in vv. 7-12 is hard to classify, but its present position is subsequent to the rest of the chapter. Some of it is intended to be seen as the continuation and conclusion of Wisdom's speech in vv. 4-6. Verse 10 has probably been misplaced and was intended to form the conclusion of chs. 1–9.

The prologue (1.1-7) has undergone a number of changes. It probably consisted originally only of vv. 1-4 and formed an introduction to an instruction or series of instructions at an early stage of composition. Subsequently vv. 5 and 6 were added to give a wider application, both in respect of readership and contents, to following material; at this stage some of the other parts of the book such as the proverbs in chs. 10ff. were included. Finally, 1.7 and 9.10 were inserted to create a framework embracing the whole of chs. 1–9, possibly as prologue and epilogue to them as an independent work, but more probably to mark them out as an extended 'introduction' to the whole book of Proverbs.

In sum, the history of the composition of these chapters cannot be traced with certainty; but the above analysis represents a reasonable possibility. These chapters may contain both old and late material (none of it precisely datable). Their earliest core was a series of instructions given by fathers to their sons with a short preface. How many of these were included in the earliest collection cannot be determined; but other material of various kinds accumulated over a fairly long period of time, including poems deriving from a somewhat different tradition in which wisdom was not a common noun but was presented in personified form as a female figure. Almost all of these additions were appended to or inserted into the original instructions, although some of them—the wisdom poems—bear the marks of having originally had an independent existence. Other additions were made to remind the readers that the aim of human teaching should be to instil the 'fear of Yahweh' in the pupil, a point which had been insufficiently stressed in the earlier stages. These wisdom additions and Yahweh additions, however, were made sporadically and not necessarily in connection with one another. Chapter 9 was then appended to the whole. Finally the prologue was expanded to make its scope more comprehensive, and chs. 1–9 became an extended introduction to the whole book.

Chapter 2

PROVERBS 10.1–22.16 AND 25–29

These chapters consist almost entirely of short (two-line, single-verse) proverbs (henceforward referred to as the 'sentence literature'). Of these, the great majority are self-contained sense units which, like the proverbs of other nations, were originally independent of one another; they are examples of the traditional lore or 'wisdom' of ordinary people, mainly small farmers who lived in the towns and villages of ancient Israel. The present study, however, is not concerned with the origins and background of these individual proverbs, a question which I have dealt with in a previous volume.[1] Rather, its concern is with the process which led to their present arrangement in the two great collections of the book of Proverbs, 10.1–22.16 and chs. 25–29.[2]

For many years scholars failed to discover any principle of arrangement of the proverbs except in a few short passages; and it was concluded that they had been assembled without any regard for the order in which they were placed. It was then believed that the other known proverb collections from the ancient Near East similarly lacked any specific arrangement; it has since been shown that this was

1. R.N. Whybray, *Wealth and Poverty in the Book of Proverbs* (JSOTSup, 99; Sheffield: JSOT Press, 1990), pp. 11-61.

2. The social background of the material in these two collections is basically the same. Although, as will be argued below, different emphases and interests are to be found in different chapters, attempts such as that of U. Skladny (*Die ältesten Spruchsammlungen in Israel* [Göttingen: Vandenhoeck & Ruprecht, 1962]) and others to discover basically different social settings for different groups of chapters have not proved convincing. The reasons for the positions of these two collections in the book in its final form will be discussed in the final chapter of the present volume.

not always the case,[3] although some scholars continue to hold the earlier view.[4]

It was G. Boström[5] who in 1928 first began to investigate the possibility that some of the proverbs in these chapters might have been placed together because they possess some common features. Boström's study was, however, limited in scope: he restricted it to the phenomenon of paronomasia or wordplay, more specifically similarities of *sound*, and to pairs of immediately adjacent verses; and he did not investigate the question of possible affinities of *sense* or topic.

It was not until 1968, with the publication of H.-J. Hermisson's work on the 'proverb wisdom' (*Spruchweisheit*) of ancient Israel,[6] that the investigation of the composition of these chapters really began. Hermisson, however, in a work mainly concerned with other aspects of the material, devoted only a few pages to a detailed examination of a possible *Ordnungselement*, and analysed only six chapters: chs. 10–15. He used both formal and thematic criteria, and concluded that these chapters contain a number of fairly small *Gruppierungen* consisting of two or more verses. But there was no consistent *Ordnungsprinzip* to be found there, and none was to be expected; some of the material consisted of 'isolated' proverbs, unrelated to their present contexts. The formation of the groups did not necessarily presuppose an editor or redactor: Hermisson suggested, on the analogy of Ben Sira and the Egyptian 'instructions', that author and editor were the same: the groups were not assembled from popular proverbs; rather, the fact that they were combined skilfully suggested a learned milieu for their composition. In his

---

3. See, e.g., W.G. Lambert, *Babylonian Wisdom Literature* (Oxford: Clarendon Press, 1960), pp. 213, 225; E.I. Gordon, *Sumerian Proverbs* (New York: Greenwood Press, 1968), p. 19; M. Lichtheim, *Late Egyptian Wisdom Literature in the International Context* (OBO, 52; Freiburg [Switzerland]: Universitätsverlag; Göttingen: Vandenhoeck & Ruprecht, 1983), pp. 63-65.

4. So W. McKane, *Proverbs: A New Approach* (OTL; London: SCM Press, 1970), p. 10, who speaks of 'the random way in which sentences follow one upon another in any chapter'.

5. G. Boström, *Paronomasi i den äldre hebreiska maschallitteraturen med särskild hänsyn till Proverbia* (LUÅ, NS I/23/8; Lund: Gleerup; Leipzig: Otto Harrassowitz, 1928).

6. H.-J. Hermisson, *Studien zur israelitischen Spruchweisheit* (WMANT, 28; Neukirchen–Vluyn: Neukirchener Verlag, 1968), pp. 172-83.

formal analysis Hermisson was concerned to stress the element of subjectivity, due partly to the difference between ancient and modern ideas of thematic affinity.

Subsequent investigations, like that of Hermisson, were confined to only a small proportion of the material. O. Plöger in an article published in 1971[7] dealt only with ch. 11. G.E. Bryce in 1972 investigated ch. 25.[8] He was the first to postulate the existence of a large-scale, independent work within the larger collection: the whole of ch. 25, with the exception of the final verse, was a single independent 'wisdom book', an instruction for courtiers, comparable with some of the Egyptian 'instructions'. In an article that appeared in 1979[9] I concentrated on the investigation of those proverbs which refer by name to Yahweh, concluding that these had in some instances been employed as the nucleus in the formation of small groups of proverbs to which they gave a new interpretation. T. Hildebrandt[10] in 1988 discussed the formation of 'proverbial pairs', but did not postulate the existence of larger groups. In all these studies the thematic criterion played a major role. R.C. Van Leeuwen,[11] also in 1988, analysed chs. 25–27, employing *inter alia* structuralist methods; he reached a conclusion similar to that of Bryce with regard to ch. 25 and also found three major 'proverb poems' in ch. 26, but was unable to discover a literary unity in ch. 27, which he called simply a 'proverb miscellany'. J. Krispenz (1989)[12] discovered thirteen examples of larger units in chs. 10–29; it is not clear whether she considers these to be the only examples of the genre, or whether she

7.   O. Plöger, 'Zur Auslegung der Sentenzensammlungen des Proverbiabuches', in H.W. Wolff (ed.), *Probleme biblischer Theologie: Gerhard von Rad zum 70. Geburtstag* (Munich: Kaiser Verlag, 1971), pp. 402-16.

8.   G.E. Bryce, 'Another Wisdom-"Book" in Proverbs', *JBL* 91 (1972), pp. 145-57.

9.   R.N. Whybray, 'Yahweh-Sayings and their Contexts in Proverbs 10.1–22.16', in M. Gilbert (ed.), *La sagesse de l'Ancien Testament* (BETL, 51; Gembloux: Duculot; Leuven: Leuven University Press, 1979), pp. 153-65.

10.   T. Hildebrandt, 'Proverbial Pairs: Compositional Units in Proverbs 10–29', *JBL* 107 (1988), pp. 207-24.

11.   R.C. Van Leeuwen, *Context and Meaning in Proverbs 25–27* (SBLDS, 96; Atlanta: Scholars Press, 1988).

12.   J. Krispenz, *Spruchkompositionen im Buch Proverbia* (Europäische Hochschulschriften, 349; Frankfurt: Peter Lang, 1989).

offers them merely as illustrations of her method.

Systematic analysis of *all* the material in these chapters in an attempt to uncover the entire process of composition has thus only recently begun; but future commentaries will be obliged to take this aspect of the material seriously. Both the commentary by Plöger (1984)[13] and the first volume of a new commentary by A. Meinhold (1991)[14] make it an important feature of their study.

Plöger, following up his earlier analysis of ch. 11, is extremely cautious about drawing conclusions with regard to the composition of these chapters. With respect to the first main collection (10.1–22.16) he remarks that we can know virtually nothing about the aims of those who first committed these proverbs, which originally existed in oral form, to writing, or about their methods of composition. In his Introduction (p. 118) he speaks only of 'occasional' links, both verbal and thematic, between pairs of adjacent proverbs; but in the commentary itself he goes further, treating together more extensive groups, though often with some hesitation. On a larger scale, he follows earlier scholars in pointing out a formal distinction between chs. 10–15 and 16.1–22.16, the earlier chapters consisting mainly of antithetical proverbs, whereas in the later ones this feature is no longer prominent, an indication of the existence of two originally separate collections despite the fact that there is no explicit sign of this in the text. Similarly in chs. 25–29 he recognizes a frequently observed difference between chs. 25–27 and 28–29, noting, apart from other considerations, that while chs. 28–29 and especially ch. 29 contain some Yahweh proverbs, this type of proverb is found hardly at all in chs. 25–27. He believes, however, that the heading in 25.1, referring to the editorial work of the 'men of Hezekiah', should be taken as covering the whole of chs. 25–29, an indication that two major collections have been combined at some stage of composition to form a larger one.

Meinhold, both in the Introduction to the first volume of his commentary, in his table of contents covering the whole book and in his detailed treatment of chs. 10–15, stands at the opposite end of the

---

13. O. Plöger, *Sprüche Salomos (Proverbia)* (BKAT, 17; Neukirchen–Vluyn: Neukirchener Verlag, 1984).

14. A. Meinhold, *Die Sprüche*. I. *Sprüche Kapitel 1–15* (Zürcher Bibelkommentare AT, 16.1; Zürich: Theologischer Verlag, 1991).

spectrum from McKane. For 10.1–22.16 and chs. 25–29 he postulates a series of stages of composition from the formation of pairs and triads to that of larger groups (*grössere Spruchgruppen*) and then to sections or paragraphs (*Abschnitte*), which have been further developed into chapters and thence into sub-collections (*Teilsammlungen*: 10–15; 16.1–22.16; 25–27; 28–29) and finally to the *Hauptsammlungen* or main collections (10.1–22.16; 25–29). Almost every verse is seen as part of an *Abschnitt*. These *Abschnitte* are generally marked out by introductory and concluding verses. Although formal and verbal links played a considerable part in their formation, Meinhold feels able to give to each a title which describes its character in terms of thematic content. A full assessment of Meinhold's methods must await the appearance of his second volume; but from his detailed treatment of chs. 10–15 it is already clear that he envisages the aim of the *Abschnitte* as an educational one, and also that he attributes an important role to Yahweh proverbs in the formation of those groups in which they occur.

Compositional Criteria

The present study starts from the assumption that with very few exceptions each of the short proverbs in these chapters—in almost every case consisting of a single verse in modern Bibles—was originally an independent, self-contained unit existing in oral form, and that they have subsequently been committed to writing and assembled into collections, presumably for the edification of readers. These collections pose two interrelated problems: whether it is possible to discern any significance in the order in which the individual proverbs are now arranged, and, if this is the case, by what criteria it may be possible to postulate the existence of deliberately organized groups of proverbs.

Broadly speaking, only two such criteria are available: identity or affinity of sense, and identity or affinity of sound (what is known as paronomasia, that is, assonance, alliteration, rhyme and wordplay in general, but also including verbal repetition). This phenomenon does not necessarily imply oral composition, nor is it necessarily mnemonic in nature: all written poetry is (in theory) intended to be read aloud, and reading aloud was a universal custom in the ancient world. Even in modern poetry when it is read silently the unvoiced sounds play an important part in its appreciation and effects on the reader.

The difficulty in discerning connections between adjacent proverbs lies in the *application* of these criteria. With regard to the criterion of sense, the critic is dealing mainly with probabilities rather than with certainties. We cannot be certain—quite apart from the obscurities of meaning which we encounter when attempting to interpret many of these proverbs—what ideas would have seemed congruous to an ancient author or editor: we are to a large extent ignorant of the processes of ancient logic, and are for the most part thrown back, *faute de mieux*, on our own, modern way of thinking, which may not always be to the point.

With regard to affinities of sound, the drawing of conclusions is even more hazardous. The possibility of sheer coincidence is enormous. The Hebrew alphabet contains only twenty-two letters; that one or more of these might recur in a pair or a succession of verses by pure chance cannot be dismissed. Arguments based on the repetition of certain vowels or combinations of vowels are even more fragile, not only because there are after all only a handful of vowels, but also because the ancient pronunciation of Hebrew vowels is uncertain.

The same difficulty applies to the repetition of words: not only is the vocabulary employed in the book of Proverbs limited, but it is also specialized: many key words, and others too, occur over and over again throughout the book; and, once again, even a purely random arrangement of proverbs could undoubtedly produce repetition of such words in adjacent verses, or even sometimes in larger groups. The same applies to such phenomena as adjacent proverbs beginning with the same letter, or even with the same word.

This is, however, by no means to deny that verses or groups of verses may have been deliberately linked in any or all of such ways. But the two criteria must be applied with caution and a sense of proportion—in other words, with common sense. Perhaps the most useful test which should be applied is that of *frequency* of repetition. If—to choose an obvious example—a whole series of verses is concerned with a single topic such as fools or kings, and especially if the same key word appears in all, or nearly all, of them, it is difficult to deny that these proverbs have been deliberately collected to form a group. The combination of the phenomenon of affinity of sense with that of sound obviously strengthens such a conclusion, though this is not always present and is not essential to this conclusion. What is fatal to any investigation of the phenomena is to begin with the *presupposition* that the material contains no 'isolated' proverbs: that it must be forced, willy-nilly, into some kind of group.

It must also be recognized that there may be groups of more than one kind. It is clear that, with few exceptions, these chapters do not contain closely knit, structured poems like those found in chs. 1–9 and 31.1-31. Whatever groups are to be found here are necessarily of a looser kind, since they are literary constructions made up from originally separate, short proverbs. Some groups, indeed, may be more loosely organized than others: a chapter or part of a chapter may, for example, group together proverbs on a number of different topics, yet be, in some sense, a 'group'; it may have been intended to be (though in a looser sense than the instructions of chs. 1–9) an 'instruction' setting out various principles of conduct which a father or teacher wished to inculcate in a pupil, or which were seen by an editor (as is the case with some of the laws of the Old Testament such as the Decalogue) to sum up Yahweh's requirements of his worshippers. Such a hypothesis is, however, more plausible if some indication of this, such as a clear introduction or summarizing conclusion, can be found, or if a Yahweh proverb—or more than one—can be seen to have an important function within the group.

Compositional Types

A great variety of methods and devices has been employed to link one proverb with another and to form larger groups. But we begin our investigation with the composition of the smallest unit, the individual proverb.

It was first suggested by O. Eissfeldt in 1913[15] that some of the proverbs in these chapters are themselves composite: that they originally consisted of a single line to which a second line was subsequently added. This theory was closely connected with his view of the difference between the popular proverb (*Volksspruch*) and the literary or consciously artistic proverb (*Kunstspruch*). In their present form the proverbs in these chapters were to be classified as *Kunstsprüche*; but in many cases a short popular proverb had been converted into a

15. O. Eissfeldt, *Der Maschal im Alten Testament* (BZAW, 24; Giessen: Töpelmann, 1913).

Kunstspruch by the addition of an appropriate second line.

Eissfeldt produced a number of arguments to support his theory. He drew attention to the curious phenomenon that in a number of instances a first line of a proverb occurs more than once, each time completed by a different second line, suggesting that the same popular proverb—which is not always or necessarily in poetic form—has been 'capped' in different ways by different literary persons. He pointed out that such 'popular' first lines are complete in themselves, making complete statements, and also argued that they have their own stylistic characteristics: they are terse and vivid as would be expected in popular proverbs, and have a predilection for assonance and/or alliteration, for example:

11.2a	*bāʾ zādôn wayyābōʾ qālôn*	When pride comes, then comes disgrace.
13.3a	*nōṣēr pîw šōmēr napšô*	He who guards his mouth keeps his life.

A further not very convincing point made by Eissfeldt is that popular proverbs are concerned with matters of general human interest—a feature in fact certainly not exclusive to this kind of proverb as found in the book of Proverbs.

There has been much subsequent critical discussion of Eissfeldt's thesis.[16] Apart from the problematic nature of his distinction between the *Volksspruch* and the *Kunstspruch*, it is now clear that alliteration and assonance are not confined to the single line but extend to whole proverbs and, beyond the individual proverb, to adjacent ones. The discussion has, however, not led to a consensus of opinion, and the question remains open. In some cases, for example in 11.2, there

16. E.g., C. Westermann ('Weisheit im Sprichwort', in K.-H. Bernhardt [ed.], *Schalom: Studien zu Glaube und Geschichte Israels, Alfred Jepsen zum 70. Geburtstag* [Stuttgart: Calwer Verlag, 1971], pp. 73-85, = *Forschung am Alten Testament: Gesammelte Studien* [TBü, AT, 55; Munich: Chr. Kaiser Verlag, 1974], II, pp. 149-61, n. 2 and again in *Wurzeln der Weisheit: Die ältesten Sprüche Israels und anderer Völker* [Göttingen: Vandenhoeck & Ruprecht, 1990], pp. 51-52) and J.M. Thompson (*The Form and Function of Proverbs in Ancient Israel* [The Hague: Mouton, 1974], pp. 66-67) tend to accept Eissfeldt's position. On the other hand, Hermisson (*Studien*, pp. 40-64), followed by G. von Rad (*Weisheit in Israel* [Neukirchen–Vluyn: Neukirchener Verlag, 1970], pp. 42-44, ET *Wisdom in Israel* [London: SCM Press, 1972], pp. 26-28) and H.D. Preuss (*Einführung in die alttestamentliche Weisheitsliteratur* [Stuttgart: Kohlhammer, 1987], p. 37), regards the proverbs in these chapters as essentially 'school wisdom' with little or no basis in popular proverbial sayings.

appears to be some justification for Eissfeldt's view: the first line of this verse hardly constitutes a poetical line but has its own distinctive rhythm; it has strongly marked assonance and also rhyme; it has some affinity with prose popular sayings such as are found scattered in the narrative and prophetical books of the Old Testament; it makes a complete statement which requires no further elaboration; and its style is quite different from that of the second line in which there is no assonance but which somewhat tritely matches it with a corresponding antithetical statement that 'with the humble is wisdom'. Such judgments, however, remain speculative; and in general it is probably best to take the two-line proverbs as the basic unit in these chapters.[17]

Proverb Pairs
In many instances two proverbs appear to have been juxtaposed in order to form pairs. Some of these pairs have no common theme but are linked only by verbal repetition or by affinities of sound (paronomasia). The frequency of occurrence of this latter phenomenon has, however, been exaggerated—the fact that only twenty-two letters are available for the formation of Hebrew words, referred to above, is relevant here. Some examples of dubious validity may be given. For example, in 12.22 and 23 the occurrence together in both verses of *q* and *r* (*šāqer*, 'falsehood', v. 22; *yiqrā'*, 'proclaims',[18] or in 13.12 and 13 of the letters *ḥ*, *l* and *b* (not in the same order!— *maḥᵃlāh-lēb*, 'makes the heart sick', v. 12; *yēḥābel-lô*, 'will be ruined', v. 13[19]) is not sufficiently striking to be significant, nor does *bôṭēaḥ*, 'trusting', in 11.28 immediately call to mind *ṭôb*, 'good', in 11.27.[20]

Krispenz also finds paronomasia linking verses which are separated from one another by several intervening verses. For example, she considers that the occurrence of *'erek* ('long') in 15.18 and of *'ōraḥ*, 'path' in 15.24 marks the beginning and end respectively of a distinct

17. Hermisson accepts that some of the proverbs contain lines which have the *form* of popular proverbs, but doubts whether such lines ever had popular currency; they are probably as much the creation of learned writers as the accompanying lines. If that were so, there would be no reason to suppose that the two lines ever existed separately.

18. Boström, *Paronomasi*, p. 138.

19. Boström, *Paronomasi*, p. 141.

20. Krispenz, *Spruchkompositionen*, p. 166.

group; similarly, *yaśkîl*, 'succeeds', in 17.8 is echoed by *kᵉsîl*, 'fool', in 17.12. This is improbable unless it can be established that between such pairs there stretches a continuous chain of paronomasia joining the two; and this Krispenz has not succeeded in demonstrating (there are disconcerting errors of fact in the tables which she presents of these passages on pp. 170, 173). It must be considered a principle that the greater the distance in a text between supposedly corresponding words, the less probable it is that their resemblance is anything other than coincidence. It is extremely unlikely that either auditors or readers would be able to retain a memory or echo of what they had heard or read for more than a very short time. Any connection between the members of such a supposed 'pair' would therefore remain unobserved.

It may also be remarked that unusual, and so particularly striking, words are more likely to be effective as paronomasia (as distinct from simple repetition of the same word) than are more common words, which are less memorable. So, for example, in 18.1 and 2 the similarity between the words *yitgallā‘* ('quarrels', v. 1) and *bᵉhitgallôt*('in expressing his opinion', v. 2)—words which are from different roots and are totally unconnected semantically—is sufficiently striking to have drawn these two verses together to form a pair.

There is a difference between paronomasia and the repetition of identical words. The latter phenomenon frequently expresses an identity of theme; but it may also occur as a means of linking together two verses which have no thematic connection, for example in 14.12 and 13, both of which contain the word *’aḥᵃrît*, 'end'. More commonly, however, there is a sense link in that the repeated word is a key word; that is, it announces the *topic* with which a verse—or, in some cases, a line—is concerned. Such key words are of course often the basis of the formation of larger groups such as those linked by 'fool', 'lazy person', 'king'.

There is also a difference between topic and theme: identity of topic is not always a pointer to identity of thought or attitude. Thus pairs or groups linked by key words may consist of proverbs whose only connection is the key word. For example, in 25.2-7, proverbs which are all concerned with kings, the two double proverbs vv. 4-5 and 6-7 have no common theme although they have a common topic: the first deals with the bad influence of wicked advisers to the king, while the second merely uses the imagery of the royal court to recommend modesty in the presence of superiors.

The use of similar imagery can also constitute a link between verses. So 25.25 and 26, where there is a common form but no thematic link, have clearly been juxtaposed because both use imagery relating to water and its fitness or unfitness for drinking. Prov. 25.18 and 19, also similes, employ imagery denoting something which is disagreeable or dangerous—although in this case there is also a slight thematic connection in that both verses are warnings against unsatisfactory neighbours.

By far the most frequent element in the formation of pairs is a common theme, whether accompanied by paronomasia or word repetition or not. In some cases, as in 18.6 and 7, the same thought is simply expressed twice with no progression of thought. More frequently, however, there is some kind of progression or development. This may take several forms: one proverb may explain the meaning of another, it may correct or modify it, it may extend or develop its thought, it may offer a concrete example of the general principle expressed in it, or it may even specifically contradict it.

Instances of a general proverb glossed by a more concrete one are frequent. For example, while 10.4 speaks generally of the consequences of laziness and diligence, 10.5 illustrates that thought quite concretely with the example of two sons: one who willingly helps with the harvest and one who is too lazy to do anything about it. Again, while 15.2 refers in general terms to wise and foolish speech, 15.1 shows how speech can be used and what consequences it may have: to appease or to enrage an interlocutor.

In other cases a proverb may serve to extend the thought of its neighbour. While 11.10 states that the inhabitants of a city have cause for joy in the prosperity of the righteous and the downfall of the wicked, v. 11 probes deeper and makes the additional point that their prosperity *depends* on that of the righteous and that the wicked, if unchecked, have the power to destroy the community altogether. Prov. 14.20 and 21 are linked by the close similarity of their opening words (*gam-lᵉrē'ēhû; bāz-lᵉrē'ēhû*), but also by the fact that v. 21 makes a judgment on the state of affairs reported in v. 20: it is not only an unfortunate fact that the poor are hated while the rich are popular; such an attitude towards the poor is wrong, and generosity towards them will be rewarded. In this case the second proverb is a comment only on the first half of the previous verse.

Prov. 16.18 and 19 also are linked both by their vocabulary and by a common theme. *gōbah rûaḥ* in v. 18, 'haughtiness of spirit', finds its opposite in *šᵉpal-rûaḥ*, 'humble of spirit', in v. 19, and *gā'ôn*, 'pride', in v. 18 is reflected in *gē'îm*, 'the proud', in v. 19. The general purport of the two verses is the same; but whereas v. 18, a synonymous proverb, speaks only of the ultimate downfall of the proud, v. 19, an antithetical proverb, makes the implication explicit, directly advocating humility.

Prov. 17.1 and 2 are both concerned with family life; but they regard it from different points of view. It cannot be said that either proverb constitutes an extension of the thought of the other; but it is unlikely that, despite the lack of repetition of any word, juxtaposition of these two proverbs should have been accidental. In fact the word *rîb*, 'strife', which concludes v. 1, may have provided the specific link between them, since v. 2, which envisages a situation in which an unsatisfactory son is replaced as heir to the family property by a competent servant, must imply the existence of a quarrel within the family. It should be noted that the link is only between v. 2 and the second line of v. 1: the first line of that verse is ignored. This phenomenon, whereby one verse fastens on to only half of another, sometimes not the most significant one, is fairly frequent in these chapters.

Prov. 19.11 and 12 are both concerned with anger. Verse 12 refers to the awesome power of kings, whose anger is terrifying but whose favour gives delight (and probably advancement) to its recipients. Verse 11 does not specifically mention kings, but is clearly applicable to them. The relationship between the two proverbs is thematic, not verbal: different words for 'anger' are used (*'ap, za'ap*). Verse 11 proposes a modification of the harsh references in v. 12 to the king's anger: good sense or insight may dictate the restraint of anger, and the overlooking of faults is a mark of nobility of character.

Prov. 20.5 and 6 are concerned with the problem of discerning the character or intentions of others. (There is a verbal link here in that the word *'îš*, 'a man', occurs twice in each verse.) Verse 6, taking the specific example of trustworthiness, states (by means of the question 'Who can find...?') that it is impossible to find (*māṣā'*) a trustworthy person: this probably means that such persons do not exist, rather than that the task of finding one is an impossible one. Verse 5, however, gives a different nuance to the line by taking it in the latter sense: it discusses the question in more general terms, asserting that although the thoughts of the human mind are well hidden, like deep water, they can be discovered (*dālâ*, 'to draw out', preserving the water metaphor) by a person of intelligence. Verse 5 thus substitutes the notion of the efficacy of the possession of wisdom for the more negative attitude of v. 6.

Prov. 20.20 and 21 are related in a variety of ways. Verse 21, about the 'hasty' acquisition of family property, probably implies some kind of deception or violence by means of which a son manages to deprive his parents of their possessions. Verse 20 goes further: here a son is described as *cursing* his parents. It also warns of much more severe consequences: whereas in v. 21 it is merely said that the son's action 'will not be blessed', v. 20 asserts his total annihilation: his 'lamp will be quenched'. But there is also another link between the two proverbs: the one who curses (v. 20) will not be blessed (v. 21). It is implied in both proverbs that it is Yahweh who will carry out the punishments.

There are some difficulties in the interpretation of 27.5 and 6,[21] but they clearly have the common topic of friendship (*'ᵃhābâ*, 'love', v. 5; *'ôhēb*, 'friend', v. 6) and express similar thoughts. Both are concerned to point out the importance of frankness in the relationship: to rebuke (*tôkaḥat*, v. 5) a friend when he is in the wrong, or even to 'wound' him (*peṣa'*, v. 6) may be necessary, and is in fact to perform a service to him. Verse 6 appears to be intended to clarify the meaning of v. 5, which is somewhat vague, although no doubt it was clear enough in its original context, stressing the fact that to rebuke friends when they deserve it—even to 'wound' them—should not impair the relationship but is of the very nature of true friendship: it is 'faithful' (*ne'ᵉmān*). Verse 6 also carries the point further by warning that one should beware of those who overdo endearments ('kisses!'), for these may conceal hidden enmity.

The best known and most obvious pair of proverbs in the book is 26.4 and 5. Each consists not of a statement but an admonition, the

---

21. In v. 5 the sense of *mᵉsuttāret* is disputed; but the context suggests the meaning 'hidden' (cf. LXX). In the second line of v. 6 *na'tārôt* is obscure; but some contrast with *ne'ᵉmānîm*, 'faithful', in the first line is evidently intended. LXX has 'willing' or 'spontaneous'. N.B. These notes on textual and exegetical problems are not intended to be full discussions. The commentaries should be consulted.

first negative and the second positive, followed by a motive clause
(*pen-*, 'lest...'). The first lines contradict one another: 'Do not answer
('*al-ta'an*)'; 'Answer (*'anēh*)'. Unfortunately it is not entirely clear
what is meant by 'answering a fool according to his folly'
(*kᵉ'iwwaltô*), the effect of which would be, according to v. 4, to make
the answerer himself a fool but, according to v. 5, to make the fool
think himself a wise man. Each proverb appears to be complete in
itself; but in their present juxtaposition one is almost certainly
intended as a correction of the other, and it is the warning of v. 4
which is most likely to correct the positive recommendation of v. 5.
The stated reason for answering the fool 'according to his folly' in
v. 5 is to prevent him from considering himself wise. This suggests
that one ought to point out his folly to him. Verse 4, however, warns
that if one does so one may oneself become a fool like him. This
suggests that in this proverb to answer him 'according to his folly'
means to take him seriously even though one suspects that he is a
fool—that is, to give him the benefit of the doubt, and to act on what
he proposes; this would indeed be utterly foolish. Whether the above
is a correct interpretation of this pair of proverbs or not, the placing
of them together as a pair is certainly intended to provoke thought.

Instructional Pairs. Scattered through these chapters are a number of
verses which employ the same terminology and sometimes the same
form as the introductory sections of the instructions in chs. 1–9. It
will be demonstrated below that these have played a significant role in
the formation of more extensive groups of proverbs. But in one case
at least it seems that such an 'instructional' verse has been combined
with a single proverb to form a pair. Prov. 19.27 is an admonition
addressed to 'my son' (*bᵉnî*), urging him to 'listen to instruction'
(*lišmōa' mûsār*) and not to stray from 'words of knowledge' (*'imᵉrê-
dā'at*). This verse corresponds exactly with the parental admonitions
in chs. 1–9 such as 1.8 and 4.1. It does not appear, however, to
introduce a more specific instruction, although v. 28, a warning
against perjury, would be appropriate as an item of parental teaching.
A connection with the *preceding* verse (26) is more probable. The
condemnation of the disgraceful behaviour of a son (*bēn*) towards his
parents in v. 26 appears to have been seen as an extreme example of a
failure to heed parental teaching and so to have attracted to itself the
otherwise isolated admonition by a parent to a son (*bᵉnî*) of v. 27.

In other cases verses of instructional material have been combined to form pairs. Prov. 15.31 and 32 both speak of the reception (or rejection) of instruction ('The ear that heeds life-giving instruction [*'ōzen šōma'at tôkaḥat ḥayyîm*] will abide among the wise [*b^eqereb ḥ^akāmîm tālîn*']', v. 31; ignoring instructions [*mûsār*], 'hearing instruction' [*tôkaḥat*], v. 32). Verse 31 is entirely positive; but v. 32, an antithetical proverb, adds a negative warning. The thought of this pair has been further extended by the addition of a third verse which identifies this instruction in wisdom (*mûsar ḥokmâ*) with the fear of Yahweh (v. 33a).

Prov. 13.13 and 14 also employ the terminology of the instruction. 'Word' (*dābār*) and 'commandment' (*miṣwâ*) here (v. 13) refer, as in the instructions of chs. 1–9, to the 'teaching of the wise' (*tôrat ḥākām*) in v. 14, not to the law of Yahweh; but it may have been the ambiguity of these terms which was felt to need the definition which v. 14 gives of them. But v. 14 also clarifies the meaning of the 'reward' promised in v. 13b to those who 'fear the commandment': this is nothing less than 'a fountain of life'.

Pairs Formed with Yahweh Proverbs. Of the sixty-one verses in these chapters in which the name Yahweh occurs, many clearly form thematic pairs—or, in some cases, triads and short groups—with adjacent 'non-Yahweh' proverbs. In each case the main purpose of the pairing seems to have been to match a proverb which speaks of the fate of a particular type of person without reference to God with one which states clearly that it is Yahweh himself who controls such persons' fate. At the same time the Yahweh proverb sometimes puts the matter on a new level.

In this way the Yahweh proverb 10.3 picks up the statement of v. 4, that poverty is the result of laziness and wealth of diligence, asserting that the real cause of poverty has to do with moral conduct rather than with a lack of energy and, more importantly, that Yahweh will protect the righteous from it while seeing to it that the wicked are thwarted in their desire for wealth. This verse is also, however, probably intended as a comment on v. 2, which refers to 'treasures gained by wickedness' and to the security given to the righteous.

Prov. 10.27-28 and 10.29-30 are two pairs each with a Yahweh component (vv. 27, 29). They have probably been placed together to form a larger group. All four verses share the common theme of the respective fates of the righteous or upright and the wicked. Verses 27 and 28 are concerned with human hopes and expectations; v. 27 equates the righteous with those who fear Yahweh and promises not only joy to them and disappointment to the wicked, but a long life for the former and a short one for the latter. With regard to the second pair, v. 29 expresses the same thought about the fates of the righteous and the wicked as does v. 30, but in terms of 'the way of Yahweh'.

Prov. 11.19 and 20 also deal in general terms with the fates of righteous and wicked; but while for v. 19 these are 'life' and 'death' respectively, v. 20 speaks rather of the 'delight' or favour and the abomination' of Yahweh. Here again there appears to be a triad rather than only a pair, with the Yahweh proverb placed in the centre: v. 21 gives an assurance of the punishment of the wicked and the deliverance of the righteous. There may also be a connection with v. 18.

Prov. 15.16 and 17 are closely similar in form as well as in theme. Each makes a comparison and in the same terms: 'Better (*ṭôb*) is X...than (*min-*) Y'; and in each case a necessitous but virtuous mode of life is compared favourably with one that is luxurious but troubled by dissension. The main difference between the two verses is that v. 16 names the fear of Yahweh as the positive feature which outweighs the advantages of wealth and gives happiness to those who only have 'a little', whereas v. 17 speaks of an affectionate family relationship ('love'). Here again a third proverb may be involved: v. 15 states that although poverty brings great material hardship, a cheerful heart is a continuous feast—a thought perhaps reminiscent of the 'little' of v. 16 and the 'fatted ox' of v. 17.

Prov. 18.10-11 is also an obvious pair. These verses share a substantial amount of vocabulary: *'ōz*, 'strength', in the phrases *migdal-'ōz*, 'strong tower', v. 10; *qiryat 'uzzô*, 'his strong city', v. 11, and also the term *niśgāb*, 'safe, high' in both verses. The topic also is the same: both are concerned with what can best be relied on as a protection from danger. But the two proverbs give quite different answers to this question: whereas for v. 11 it is wealth which is the best protection, for v. 10 it is 'the name of Yahweh', and is only available to the righteous.

Prov. 19.20-21 also has a common key word: *'ēṣâ*, 'advice', v. 20; 'plan, purpose', v. 21. Here again the Yahweh proverb modifies, or even annuls, the thought of the other. Verse 20 is a characteristic wisdom admonition, recommending the heeding (*šāma'*) of advice and the acceptance of human (presumably parental) teaching as the means to acquire wisdom, which will lead a person to success throughout life. Verse 21, however, points out that human plans are entirely dependent on Yahweh: it is his will or purpose (*'ēṣâ*) which will always prevail.

Prov. 20.26 speaks of the wise king who is sufficiently perceptive to be able to identify the wicked in his entourage and to deal with them; but v. 27, although it makes no direct reference to kings, asserts that it is Yahweh who possesses such powers of perception *par excellence*: it is he whose lamp (*nēr*) is the spirit in people which 'searches the innermost parts' of all human beings. This may mean that he gives to human beings the power of such perception, or that he uses the spirit in people which he has placed in them in order to enable him to know their thoughts. Whatever may be the correct interpretation of this line, this Yahweh proverb asserts Yahweh's control over human thoughts and actions. Verse 28, which is again about kings, may have been intended as a third element, though the connection is not very close.

Combinations of Yahweh Proverbs. In some cases Yahweh proverbs are themselves arranged in pairs or larger groups. There are four such pairs: 14.26-27; 15.8-9; 15.25-26; 29.25-26. There are two triads (20.22-24; 21.1-3), and in one case seven Yahweh proverbs follow one another to form a larger group (16.1-7). It is interesting to observe that although in some cases these groups are also connected by other common phrases (for example, 'the fear of Yahweh' in 14.26 and 27), as a rule they do not display any sequence of thought; rather, each constituent proverb refers to a different aspect of Yahweh.

Prov. 14.26 speaks of the confidence which one may derive from fearing Yahweh, while v. 27 is concerned with the benefits to be derived from this. Prov. 15.8 has the specific theme of the worship of Yahweh in sacrifice and prayer, which is acceptable only when offered by the righteous; v. 9 speaks more generally of righteous and wicked behaviour and Yahweh's reaction to these. The theme of 15.25 is also specific: Yahweh will protect the widow against those who interfere with the boundaries of her property. Verse 26, however, is a quite general statement about Yahweh's hatred of those who do evil. But there is also a possible connection with v. 27, a condemnation of the greedy. Prov. 29.25 asserts that those who trust in Yahweh will be secure; v. 26, on the other hand, is concerned with justice: Yahweh's justice is said, by implication, to be superior to that of a human ruler.

A similar apparent inconsequence characterizes the triads. Prov. 20.22 deprecates the taking of revenge: retribution should be left to Yahweh. Verse 23 is about the specific matter of commercial dishonesty with regard to false weights and measures: this is abominable to Yahweh. Verse 24 asserts that the direction of a person's life is under Yahweh's control and is hidden from the person concerned. These are all important facets of Yahweh's nature, but they are not closely interrelated. In 21.1-3 there is a connection between vv. 1 and 2, but not with v. 3. Verse 1 is about the king: his mind (*lēb*) is entirely subject to Yahweh's control; v. 2 concerns the heart or mind (*lēb*) of human beings in general, though of course applicable to kings as well as to others: Yahweh knows the human heart and assesses it (*tōkēn*). But the theme of v. 3 is only marginally related to v. 2: it asserts that righteousness and justice are more acceptable to Yahweh than sacrifice.

Yet although considered in isolation these pairs and triads of Yahweh proverbs appear to have little in common except their reference to Yahweh, it will be argued below that they are not intended to be seen in isolation but have significant roles to play in the context of larger groups of proverbs.

Conclusion. There are three possible ways in which the pairs of proverbs in these chapters could have been formed. (1) They could be the result of the editorial juxtaposition of two originally independent proverbs. (2) A single proverb could have been augmented by another composed especially to accompany it and to comment on it. (3) Two proverbs could have been simultaneously composed in order to make a pair.

It must be admitted that there can be no absolute proof how any of these pairs of proverbs was composed. It must also be observed that the proverbs are all constructed in such a way that each makes a complete, self-contained statement (or admonition), and could therefore have once existed on its own. However, it may be possible to formulate some tentative criteria concerning probabilities.

1. If the only affinity between two consecutive proverbs is purely verbal—that is, they are linked only by paronomasia or by the occurrence of the same word or words in both—it is probable that they

were originally separate proverbs, since the only reason for their juxtaposition would be an editorial one. This applies, for example, to 18.1 and 2.

2. Proverbs forming pairs which have identical or similar themes but which employ different key words are also likely to have originated separately. If there had been an original connection between them, either by simultaneous composition or by the deliberate composition of one in order to make a comment on the other, some verbal link would be expected.

3. If one proverb comments only on one line of the other, ignoring the other line, this lack of a complete 'fit' is a clear indication that both proverbs have been chosen editorially from originally separate ones. An example of this is 17.1 and 2, where v. 2, which speaks of domestic trouble, comments only on the second line of v. 1, ignoring the other. Prov. 19.11-12 is another example of this.

4. Even when it is clear that one member of a pair comments on the other by way of clarification, sequence of thought, correction and so on, this is not sufficient to prove that it was composed for that purpose or that the two were composed together. So in 15.1-2 each verse makes an individual statement and there is no verbal link. Prov. 11.10 and 11 are clearly closely connected, but the use of two different words for 'city' (*qiryâ* and *qeret*) points to different origins. Prov. 16.18 and 19 are very closely linked thematically, but even the correspondence between *gōbah rûaḥ*, 'haughty of spirit', and *šᵉpal-rûaḥ*, 'lowly of spirit', and between *gā'ôn*, 'pride', and *gē'îm*, 'proud' is insufficient to prove the modelling of one upon the other; the introduction of the topic of the poor in v. 19 indicates the contrary.

5. In the case of pairs, where one proverb is specifically instructional in character (e.g. 19.27), the special composition of the one in order to gloss or comment on the other is more probable than in the case of other pairs, since such instructional verses belong to a different type of literature from that otherwise prevailing in these chapters. Moreover, it is unlikely that such a verse should at any time have had currency as an isolated saying: elsewhere (in chs. 1–9) it is ancillary to a specific instruction; it is not the instruction itself, and is hardly conceivable as standing on its own. This is not the case, however, with the other untypical type of pair: that of which one member is a Yahweh proverb. These proverbs are self-contained statements differing from the mass of other proverbs in these chapters only in

their reference to Yahweh; and, although this difference is an important one, there is no reason to suppose that they were especially composed in order to stand in their present position.

6. There is little clear evidence of pairs of proverbs especially composed as such. Prov. 26.4 and 5, however, are probably an exception. Although it is possible that one of these proverbs was composed in order to match an already existing proverb, their total effect in leading the reader to reflect on the question which they raise, together with the very close verbal similarity and the play on the meaning of 'according to his folly' suggests that this is a single composition; and, in fact, a double proverb rather than a pair.

The above considerations are only tentative and incapable of absolute proof. But the general impression made by the study of these pairs of proverbs is that there is little evidence of 'original' editorial writing here. Almost every one of these proverbs is complete in itself; and the probability is that their pairing is the work of editors which has sometimes been carried out with great skill.

Larger Groups

The capability of the proverb for the expression of complex thoughts is strictly limited. Because it depends for its effectiveness on brevity and incisiveness, it can only make absolute statements or, if it is couched in the form of an admonition, categorical demands. It can set up antitheses, declaring one kind of person or one course of action to be good or desirable and another to be bad or undesirable, but it cannot qualify these statements or demands by, for example, proposing plausible alternatives, or by setting out two differing sides of a question. The most it can do (in the case of the proverbs with which we are dealing here) is to add the word *yēš*, 'There is/are', to a statement, indicating that it applies only to some people or situations but not to others (e.g. 11.24; 13.7; 18.24) or to use the construction *ṭôb...min-*, 'Better is/are...than' to indicate that one thing (or person, or mode of behaviour) is preferable to another (e.g. 15.17; 16.8, 19, 32; 25.24); but such qualifications do not present the hearer or reader with real alternatives: they remain categorical, and do not concede that a question may have two sides.

As we have seen, some attempts have been made to overcome the limitations of a single, isolated proverb. Some proverbs may have been made deliberately ambiguous or 'open-ended' (McKane's term), implying, for the perspicacious hearer or reader, that alternatives might exist; in other cases, a second line may have been added to a single-line proverb in order to expand a statement and to give it a somewhat broader scope. The addition of a motive clause or explanatory line giving a reason for a statement or admonition (e.g. 14.7; 21.7; 25.17; 26.25) was intended to persuade the hearer of its truth by showing it to be reasonable; but, again, such clauses could not reflect the complexity of real life in which choices have to be made between alternative lines of conduct.

The most obvious way to overcome this problem was to put together two proverbs which could illustrate or complement one another or to introduce new perspectives on a question. In one case (26.4-5) such a juxtaposition enabled an editor (or, in this case, more probably an author) to indicate the complexity of a question by offering *contrary* advice and giving a reason for each admonition. The effect of this was to provoke the reader to serious thought: the treatment of fools was shown to be a complex question which cannot be simply solved by adopting the recommendation of a single proverb.

In the texts that we possess, this device of making diametrically opposed observations in two consecutive proverbs with no attempt to give an explanation was only employed once. This would hardly be generally possible, and does clearly not adequately meet the requirement for reasoned discussion. It was, of course, possible to expand a two-line proverb into a four-line one, and there are some examples of this, for example 25.4-5, 6-7, 9-10. It was also possible to compose longer continuous pieces like the extended admonition in 27.23-27. But the main editorial method employed in these chapters of Proverbs was to preserve and collect together a body of already existing two-line proverbs, and wherever possible to combine these in meaningful groups, creating for them new contexts which might to some extent modify their original meanings, but by means of which some more solid and, at the same time, more wide-ranging body of lore would take shape.

That this process was carried out, at least in part of the material, for purposes of *instruction* is clear from the fairly numerous verses concerning children and their upbringing (e.g. 10.1, 5; 13.1; 15.5, 20; 17.25; 19.13, 26; 20.7; 28.7), sometimes addressed specifically to parents (13.24; 19.18; 29.17) and sometimes to the children themselves ('my son'; 19.27; 27.11). Some of these are couched in language identical with that of the instructions in chs. 1–9.

There is, therefore, a good case for supposing that at least some of these proverbs have been editorially put together with the express intention of creating 'instructions': not of the same kind as the instructions of chs. 1–9, which are unified poems, but in a looser sense, collections which may be very miscellaneous in content but nevertheless designed, like those in chs. 1–9, to constitute bodies of instructional material. This represents a considerable change from the original purpose of the individual proverbs, most of which taken by themselves have a much more general purpose and probably originally existed in oral form, circulating among the members of small communities.

Some of these collections are distinct from the others in that their inclusion of Yahweh proverbs shows them to be, at least in their final form (for a series of editorial stages in the composition of these chapters seems certain), specifically intended to inculcate in the pupils an awareness that obedience to Yahweh's will—or the 'fear' of Yahweh—is the central element and motivation of the moral conduct of an Israelite. As has been seen above, a similar development is discernible in chs. 1–9.

Criteria for the Identification of Groups. The criteria employed for identifying pairs of proverbs are only partly applicable for the identification of groups, and some new criteria come to the fore.

It must be stressed that absolute proof that certain sequences of proverbs at some stage constituted distinct and coherent entities is usually lacking, and that there is ample room for differences of opinion on this matter. The number of themes dealt with in these chapters is fairly small, and the possibility of chance similarities of theme is as great as in the case of pairs. With larger groups, however, evidence may be cumulative: the recurrence of a particular theme or topic, or of a particular form, in a number of consecutive proverbs constitute an a priori probability of the presence of a distinct group; and the longer the series in which such a phenomenon occurs, the more probable this conclusion becomes. (It should be noted in this connection that the extraneous presence of a single unrelated proverb in a series of otherwise coherent proverbs does not necessarily invalidate its identification as a group: the insertion of such extraneous material may have been due to a number of factors in the course of subsequent redaction.)

As in the case of pairs, the combination of formal with thematic or topical congruity constitutes a particularly strong case for group identification. For example, 10.1-5 forms a group thematically concerned with right and wrong ways to acquire an adequate livelihood; but there is also a formal pattern here. In these five anti-thetical proverbs the priority of positive and negative lines alternates: vv. 1, 3 and 5 begin with positive lines commending wisdom, righteousness and diligence, while vv. 2 and 4 begin with contrary statements about their opposites, wickedness and laziness.

Prov. 10.1-5 also offers a good example of another factor in the formation of groups: that the existence of a closely knit pair of proverbs does not preclude its forming, at the same time, part of a larger group. Thus vv. 4 and 5, both concerned with the importance of diligence (see above), constitute a pair; but they are also part of the larger group, whose limits are marked out by the similarity of v. 5 to v. 1—an 'inclusio' or literary envelope. There are numerous other examples of pairs within larger groups. Such pairs may have been formed separately before this incorporation, although this is not necessarily so.

An analysis of the material (see below)[22] shows that the groups are of various kinds. One of the most important distinctions is that between groups which have an obvious thematic or topical theme and those which are miscellaneous collections of proverbs, which apparently at some time functioned as compendia of information and/or admonitions about life and society and moral choices, which a compiler or editor deemed to be essential guides to proper conduct.

The most obvious groups are those which share a common topic, often but not always indicated by a key word: Yahweh, 16.1-9; kings 16.10-15; 25.2-7; fools, 26.1-12. Two of these groups, however (16.1-9 and 10-15) have been linked together to form a larger group which is concerned to provoke a consideration of the relationship between Yahweh and kings: vv. 9 and 10 are pivotal or linking verses which secure a smooth transition from one topic to the other.

But there are also obvious groups which have been formed because of their common formal characteristics. Chapter 25, for example,

22. Pp. 92-131.

contains a series of similes or comparisons (vv. 11-15, 18-20, 25-28) which have some topical and verbal links but whose main common characteristic is that of form.

Beginnings and Endings. It might be expected that, as with the instructions of chs. 1–9, a collection of proverbs designed to serve an instructional purpose should be prefaced by a general introduction commending the acquisition of wisdom or the importance of paying heed to instruction, and that it might possibly also have a definite conclusion of a general kind, summing up the content of the preceding verses. In fact, although this is not always the case in these chapters, there are some examples of formal beginnings and perhaps of conclusions.

Prov. 27.11 is addressed to 'my son' ($b^e n\hat{\imath}$) like the instructions of chs. 1–9; it is expressed in quite general terms, recommending the acquisition of wisdom (hkm); and it states that the father will rejoice in and benefit from the possession of such a wise son. It is inconceivable that this verse should have been thrown at random into an indiscriminate miscellany of unconnected proverbs: there must have been some connection between it and the surrounding material. With its imperative 'be wise, my son' it most clearly corresponds to the introductions in chs. 1–9, and there is good reason to see it as the beginning of a distinct series of proverbs. The topics which follow (vv. 12-22) are all suitable for a teacher's instruction. The extended admonition in vv. 23-27 was probably intended to form the conclusion. Formally these verses stand out prominently among material consisting entirely of short two-line proverbs; they are unconnected with what follows in ch. 28, and they mark what is generally agreed to be a definite break between chs. 25–27 and 28–29. It is possible, then, that 27.12-27 forms an 'instruction' in a looser sense than in chs. 1–9 but consisting nevertheless of an introduction, a series of proverbs suitable for the young, and an impressive conclusion.

Prov. 19.27, however, seems not to be the beginning of an instruction, but rather to be related to the *preceding* verses, and in particular to v. 18, which is a recommendation, not to a son but to a father, to discipline (ysr) his children while there is still hope for them.

Other verses also, though they lack the formal imperative style of the introduction to an instruction, may be seen to function in a similar way. It may be significant that this is the case with the opening verses of three chapters: 10, 12 and 13.

In ch. 10, vv. 1-5 have a common theme in that they are concerned to give instruction about right and wrong ways to acquire wealth or to earn one's livelihood. But they also have a distinct structure: the close resemblance between vv. 1 and 5—the latter being a concrete example of the former—marks out their beginning and end, while the instructional tone of v. 1 with its assertion that 'a wise son makes a glad father' (closely resembling 27.11) is unmistakable.

Prov. 12.1, which commends a love of discipline (*mûsār*) and knowledge (*da'at*) and the acceptance of rebuke (*tôkaḥat*) is a general introduction to the more specific teaching of the verses which follow. It is not clear, however, where this series ends. Chapter 13 abounds in references to education and the acquisition of wisdom. Verse 1, concerning the wise son who loves (or pays heed to: the verb has dropped out of this line)[23] discipline (*mûsār*) is very similar to both 10.1 and 12.1. Again, however, it is difficult to be certain about the conclusion of this group: there are a number of possibilities (see below).

Other examples of verses which appear to mark the beginnings of similar instructions include 15.20, whose first line is identical with 10.1, with a probable conclusion in v. 24, and 18.15, where the conclusion is uncertain. But there are many other passages which have no formal introduction, but whose contents nevertheless suggest the existence of a group created for teaching purposes. These will be discussed in detail below. In general, it may be said that there is sufficient evidence in these chapters of meaningful groupings to warrant the conclusion that they have undergone a major editorial shaping of individual proverbs for teaching purposes.

Yahweh Proverbs within Groups. It is hardly to be supposed that proverbs which speak of Yahweh should have been thrown at random into these chapters. It has been shown above that many of them have been used as comments of one kind or another on adjacent proverbs to form pairs. But in many instances they form part of larger groups, either to comment on a whole passage or to sum up the contents of such passages from a particular point of view. They do not generally

---

23. The first line in MT reads 'A wise son (is) a father's instruction'.

occur at the beginning of a group; rather it would seem that the group has been built round them, often creating concentric structures of which they are the centre.

Prov. 10.1-5 has already been discussed in terms of its forming a group. Verse 1 marks this out as an instruction; but its central point is the Yahweh proverb, v. 3. The commendation of filial wisdom in v. 1 as a source of joy and the warning against filial folly as a cause of grief are here the subject of an affirmation that these matters are in the hand of Yahweh: the acquisition of wisdom leads to a righteous life; and Yahweh will protect the righteous from hunger while preventing the wicked from seizing the supply of food. At the same time, the Yahweh proverb is relevant to the other proverbs in the group: if treasures gained by wickedness do not profit (v. 2), it is Yahweh who sees to this; if poverty and wealth are the respective consequences of laziness and diligence (v. 4), it is important to remember that economic wellbeing is a gift of Yaweh; and similarly with v. 5.

Prov. 10.25-30 (or perhaps 25-32) is a group of proverbs (v. 26 is an exception) concerned mainly with the respective fates of the righteous and the wicked; the two Yahweh proverbs (vv. 27 and 29) add a new dimension to the points which they make: if what the wicked dread and the righteous hope for will indeed come to pass (vv. 24, 28) and the wicked will be swept away by the tempest while the righteous are established for ever (v. 25), these fates are determined by Yahweh, who gives long life to those who fear him and cuts short the life of the wicked (v. 27), and whose 'way' protects the upright and destroys the evildoers (v. 29).

In a number of instances proverbs commending wisdom are glossed by Yahweh proverbs. So in ch. 12, v. 2 comments on the commendation of wisdom in v. 1, asserting that to love wisdom is not enough: it is those who use this wisdom rightly (the 'good') who will be the recipients of Yahweh's favour. The Yahweh proverb in v. 22 performs a similar function for the surrounding verses. The same is true of 14.2, placed between two proverbs commending wisdom.

In certain chapters Yahweh proverbs occupy a particularly prominent position. Chapters 15 and 16, which are central to the major complex 10.1–22.16 both literally and theologically, and which also occupy the central position in the book as a whole,[24] contain between them no less than twenty Yahweh proverbs out of a total of fifty-eight in the whole of 10.1–22.16 and 25–29. Much of ch. 15 is concerned with wisdom (vv. 2, 5, 7, 10, 12, 14, 20, 21, 22, 24, 31, 32, 33). In several instances the Yahweh proverbs stand in places relevant to the surrounding verses; but it is especially significant that immediately following two verses which commend paying heed to instruction (vv. 31-32), the chapter ends, in a manner very similar to 1.7, with the identification of this with the fear of Yahweh: 'The fear of Yahweh *is* instruction in wisdom' (v. 33), a verse which sums up and comments on what is a particularly important theme of the whole chapter.

The first half of ch. 16, with nine Yahweh proverbs in the first eleven verses, stands by itself. That these verses are closely linked with the royal proverbs which follow (vv. 10, 12, 13, 14, 15) is obvious. The intention of the editor was to link the two topics together. The predominating theme of vv. 1-9 is Yahweh's complete control over human life, as is illustrated by the close resemblance between the opening and closing verses: 'To man belong the plans of the mind, but the answer of the tongue is from Yahweh' (v. 1); 'A man's mind plans his way, but it is Yahweh who direct his steps' (v. 9). The royal proverbs in vv. 10-15 are of various kinds: most emphasize the king's power or his wisdom, but v. 12 speaks of wicked kings and stresses that the stability of the throne is based on righteousness. It is probable that this group of royal proverbs was first collected simply in view of its topic (kings), for it has no strict thematic unity. Its juxtaposition with the preceding series of Yahweh proverbs was a subsequent development: everything that is said there about human subservience to Yahweh is equally applicable to kings, and especially relevant to them in view of their temptation to abuse their power. This point is made very clear in the juxtaposition of vv. 9 and 10: it is because human conduct is directed by Yahweh that a king is divinely inspired to administer true justice. The joining of these two groups together serves a double purpose: it teaches, on the one hand, that kings rule by divine permission and are Yahweh's representatives on earth, but, on the other, that as human beings they

---

24. The Masora points out that 16.18 is the middle verse of the book.

have this authority only if they acknowledge their subordinate status and rule righteously.

This is the clearest example in these chapters of what is found elsewhere in them on a smaller scale: the part played by Yahweh proverbs in giving a particular theological character to these collections as a whole. It should, however, be noted that some chapters (13, 26 and 27) contain no Yahweh proverbs at all, and also that chs. 25–29 contain far fewer than 10.1–22.16—only six in five chapters. This may suggest that different parts of these major complexes have been edited from quite different points of view.

Other shorter examples of groups informed by Yahweh proverbs include 16.33–17.3, 20.5-12, 20.20–21.4 and 22.1-14.

Pivotal Verses. Groups of proverbs, such as those which have been identified in the preceding discussion, have evidently been formed, probably in a series of editorial stages, in a process culminating in the present text of the larger complexes 10.1–22.16 and 25–29. It is improbable that these combinations should have been made without attempts to create links between the component groups. It has already been noted that 16.1-9 and 16.10-15 have been linked together by v. 9, which acts as a kind of pivot facing in two directions, completing one group and beginning another. This conjunction of two groups served an important thematic and even theological purpose: it invited the reader to consider the relationship between two themes, those of Yahweh and of kings, and in particular to see the status of the latter in the light of the previous statements about the former. This example of a pivotal verse is not the only one.

Prov. 15.33, for example, marks the conclusion of a group concerned with instruction in wisdom, equating this with the fear of Yahweh, but also stands at the beginning of an extended group of Yahweh sayings to whose themes it is closely related. Prov. 15.24 joins together a group of verses (20-23) describing the wise and foolish with one which speaks of Yahweh's punishment of the wicked (vv. 25-27). As a transitional verse, it connects the two themes by stating that Sheol awaits those who are unwise, implying that folly and wickedness are closely connected, a point frequently made elsewhere in these proverbs.

Prov. 16.16 immediately follows a group entirely devoted to the topic of kings. It does not, however, belong to that group, but marks the beginning of another (vv. 16-23) whose main subject is wisdom. But it would be entirely appropriate to kings, who especially need wisdom in executing their function of pronouncing judgment and assessing the character of their officials or courtiers (vv. 10, 13). Verse 16 is, accordingly, a transitional verse leading from one topic to another.

Prov. 16.33 may also be a pivotal verse. On the one hand it is clearly intended to mark the conclusion of ch. 16 with a final comment which recalls the first verse of that chapter, while on the other hand it is the opening verse of the short group 16.33–17.3. Prov. 26.12 serves a similar purpose. The first part of ch. 26 is entirely devoted to the topic of fools; vv. 13-16 are concerned with the lazy. Verse 12 acts as a pivotal verse leading from one group to the other. It is connected with the preceding verses in that it speaks about fools, but is primarily concerned with persons who are 'wise in their own eyes'. These it distinguishes from fools as being wholly without hope of reformation; the meaning of this statement becomes clear only with v. 16, where it is asserted that being wise in one's own eyes is a particular characteristic of the lazy.

Looser Groupings
The groups so far identified are relatively unified. There is evidence, however, that some of the material has been rather more loosely organized into larger groups having a general tendency to concentrate on related topics, giving a tone to the whole which is not, however, necessarily exemplified in every one of the component proverbs. Such collections frequently incorporate smaller, more clearly structured groups; in some cases they correspond to whole chapters of the book as these are now constituted in modern Bibles. These larger, less strictly homogeneous groups probably represent a comparatively late stage in the composition of the major complexes. In some cases they are also distinguished by their predominant forms, such as a preponderance of one particular kind of parallelism.

Reference has already been made to one such group, ch. 16. This chapter incorporates several smaller groups which comprise almost the whole of ch. 16 and have mainly been combined for good thematic reasons. The chapter begins and ends with more or less synonymous verses (1-9, 33), which affirm that human plans and decisions are overruled by Yahweh. The chapter is also formally distinctive, consisting mainly of proverbs in synonymous parallelism.

Chapter 13 is clearly very different in intention from ch. 16. It is the only chapter in this section of the book (10.1–22.16) that lacks any reference to Yahweh. On the other hand, it has a specific character in that it is especially concerned with instruction. If, as is probable, it comprises more than one originally distinct instruction, there can be little doubt that these have been collected together in view of their common primary concern in order to form a larger collection of instructional material. It is composed predominantly of antithetical proverbs.

Chapter 15 is closely related to ch. 16 by the unusual number of Yahweh proverbs. The concentration of Yahweh proverbs in these two chapters strongly suggests that they have been placed together for this reason. It is probable that ch. 15 originally consisted of a series of shorter groups each containing one or more Yahweh proverbs. The concentration of Yahweh proverbs at the end of the chapter (four in nine verses) sums up the general tone of the chapter and also prepares for 16.1-9.

Prov. 20.20–21.4, a passage which contains seven Yahweh proverbs out of a total of fifteen verses, is a shorter group of similar character. But it may also be significant that ch. 21 as a whole (vv. 1-31) has a certain unity of its own. Its five Yahweh proverbs (vv. 1, 2, 3, 30, 31) occur at the beginning and end, enclosing the whole. These verses have a common theme: Yahweh's control over human plans and actions, a theme which is echoed (by implication) in many other verses in the chapter which speak of the frustration of the plans and actions of the wicked.

Chapter 26, in which there are no Yahweh proverbs, and which is dominated by an unusual number of proverbs in the form of similes, contains a number of groups each with a single topic: the fool (vv. 1-12), the lazy (vv. 13-16) and persons who disturb the harmony of society mainly by deceitful or malicious speech (vv. 17-28). Each is self-contained and probably once constituted a separate group; but their common concern with undesirable human types, together with their formal similarities, accounts for their subsequent combination into a larger group.

Chapter 28 clearly marks a new beginning. The previous verses (27.23-27)—an extended admonition, unique in these chapters—constitute a formal conclusion to that chapter. In ch. 28 the normal sequence of two-line (one verse) proverbs is resumed; but there is an obvious change of style: the similes and metaphors which dominate chs. 25–27 have been discarded in favour of predominantly antithetical proverbs.

In its present form ch. 28 is intended as an instruction. This is indicated by the frequency of the occurrence of the word *tôrâ*, 'teaching', four times in the first nine verses, and by the close similarity of the terms used in these verses with those used in the instructions of chs. 1–9. The chapter has no formal structure: it is a loose collection of proverbs with only occasional links between adjacent verses, and it is not certain that in its present form it should be regarded as a single instruction. But there are indications that this may be so. Almost every verse contrasts the behaviour of wicked and righteous persons, who may be thus defined as persons who ignore or reject the 'teaching' and those who keep it, often with a reference to their respective fates. It begins with a section (vv. 1-9) concerned specifically with the importance of keeping *tôrâ*, and it ends (v. 28) with a reference to the wicked and righteous and their effect on society, which appropriately constitutes a summary or conclusion. It should probably be regarded as an example of a loosely formed instruction composed of originally separate proverbs which have been made to serve as a piece of ethical and religious teaching.

Detailed Analysis

The passages discussed above are merely examples of the way in which proverbs have been grouped together in these chapters. But enough evidence has been presented to show that Prov. 10.1–22.16 and 25–29 are not random collections of unrelated independent proverbs, but that editorial processes have been at work on at least parts of the material, carried out for specific reasons. This is not to say that there is a comprehensive structure to be found here: sweeping conclusions are to be avoided, and the investigator must proceed with caution.

The links that have been established between individual proverbs and between groups of proverbs are many and varied. It is with the aim of demonstrating this in greater detail and with regard to the whole of the material that the following analysis is offered—subject, it must be emphasized, to other possible interpretations, as is evidenced by the different conclusions reached by other recent studies.

Although the problem of the composition of these chapters has recently increasingly attracted the attention of scholars, there has as yet, as already observed, been no thorough and comprehensive investigation of the whole of the material from this point of view. Plöger is the only scholar who, in his recent commentary, has paid attention throughout to the possibility of the formation of pairs and small groups. This was not, however, a main concern of his commentary, and his comments on this feature are desultory and often tentative. Meinhold in his recent commentary, of which so far only the first volume covering chs. 1–15 has become available to me, has not yet completed his analysis of the chapters under consideration here, although in his introduction he makes some general remarks about the composition of the whole book.

At the head of each section of the analysis which follows I have set out a list of those groups of proverbs which have been postulated by other scholars. Their alternative views have been taken into account; but I have not thought detailed discussion of them to be necessary or appropriate.

I have not discussed textual problems except in so far as they seriously affect the general sense of a proverb, but have based my observations on the Masoretic Text.

Chapter 10

> Hermisson 2-5, 6-9, 13-21 (22), 23-30, 31-32
> Plöger (1984), 1-5, 23-25, 31-32 (11.1)
> Krispenz 1b-7, 13-17
> Hildebrandt 15-16
> Meinhold 1-5, 6-11, 12-18, 19-21, 23-30, 31-32[25]

Several groups of greater or lesser cohesion can be discerned in this chapter. While it has no comprehensive structure marking it out as a single unit, vv. 1-5, with their emphasis on the importance of the acquisition of wisdom in childhood coupled with the reference in v. 3 to Yahweh as protector of the righteous against the greed of the wicked, may have been placed here to constitute a general introduc-

---

25. These notes, placed at the beginning of the analysis of each chapter, indicate the groupings postulated by other scholars. In some cases—especially that of Plöger—they represent no more than tentative suggestions.

tion, setting the tone for the chapter as now constituted, or indeed for more than one chapter.

Verses 1-5, to which some reference has been made above, is a closely structured group, in which each verse is related to others. The similarity between vv. 1 and 5 has already been pointed out. Verse 4 adds further precision to these verses: the consequences of the behaviour of the two kinds of son are here pointed out. Verse 3, as is so often the case with Yahweh sayings in these chapters, comments on v. 4, implying that wisdom and folly are closely related to righteous and wickedness, and stating that material wellbeing is dependent ultimately not on individual enterprise but on the will of Yahweh. But it may also be seen as a theological comment on v. 2. Taken together this group of verses is concerned with a choice which is open to everyone: a choice which once made will lead ultimately to gladness, profit, life and wealth, or to sorrow, death, hunger, poverty and shame.

There is less evidence of a common theme in vv. 6-11, although each verse (with the exception of v. 8) is concerned in some way with righteousness and/or wickedness. There are, however, verbal links between these verses. Verses 6b and 11b are identical, as also are vv. 8b and 10b.[26] The series of references to parts of the body, head, mouth (v. 6), heart (v. 8), eye, lips (v. 10), mouth (twice, v. 11), may be an example of a linking device found elsewhere in the book. There is also a possible thematic connection between vv. 6 and 7, which both speak of a 'blessing' ($b^e r\bar{a}k\hat{a}$), and between vv. 8 and 9, where v. 9 appears to interpret v. 8, setting out the concrete consequences of 'heeding the commandments'. There is also a possible connection between this group and v. 12: that verse picks up the verb *ksh* from v. 11 and could be seen as a comment on v. 11b and perhaps also on v. 10: the reprehensible actions mentioned in those verses are now correctly defined as due to hatred and a desire to stir up strife.

Verses 13-21 do not appear to form a distinct group. Verses 13-17, regarded as a thematic group by Krispenz, contain a number of verbal links between verses, but these do not extend beyond pairs of adjacent verses. Verses 14 and 15 share the word 'ruin' ($m^e hitt\hat{a}$) and vv. 16 and 17 $l^e hayy\hat{i}m$ (literally, 'to life'). Verses 13 and 14 both refer,

---

26. LXX, however, has a quite different text from MT at v. 10b.

though not in the same words, to wise and fools. There may also be paronomasia between *'āšîr/rêšām* in v. 15 and *rāšā'* in v. 16. There are also some thematic links. Verses 18-21 are all concerned with speech (lips, words, tongue). Verses 13-14 both speak of the contrast between wise and foolish speech and the consequences of these. Verse 16 comments on v. 15a, pointing out that wealth is a source of security if it is honestly gained. But these verses as a whole do not manifest a distinct pattern of thought. There is perhaps some justification for seeing vv. 18-21 as a loose group held together by the common theme of the use of speech (cf. also vv. 11, 13, 14); but again it is difficult to perceive a clear pattern. The only possible indication that vv. 13-21 might be a distinct group is the close similarity of v. 21 to v. 13, which share the phrase *ḥᵃsar lēb*, the person who lacks sense.

The Yahweh proverb v. 22 is, unlike the majority of proverbs in this chapter, not in antithetical parallelism. It appears to stand on its own. Hermisson believed that it might form the conclusion of the preceding group in view of its general character; but it seems to be unrelated to its immediate context. Its affinities, if any, are with earlier verses. In its reference to wealth it may be said to be a comment on vv. 15 and 16, making it clear that it is Yahweh who is the source of wealth. But v. 22 has clearer affinities with even earlier verses. In relation to vv. 6 and 7 it could be concerned to clarify the specific content of 'blessing', as well as to indicate its true source. But its relationship with v. 4 is clearer still. In both verses the word *taᵃšîr*, 'makes rich', occurs. The first line of v. 22 is very emphatic: 'It is the blessing of Yahweh that makes rich'; this could be a theological correction to the statement in v. 4 that it is the hand of the diligent that does this. The second line, if 'and toil does not add to it'[27] is a correct interpretation, confirms this statement. It may be—though the evidence is hardly conclusive—that the verse was inserted as a conclusion, at some point in the development of the chapter, after vv. 1-21 had been combined to form a single group.

Verses 23-32 have a common characteristic in that they make a

---

27. The subject of *lō'-yôsīp 'immāh*, literally 'does not add with it', could be either Yahweh or 'toil'. If it is the latter the meaning is probably the same as that of Ps. 127.1-2: no human effort can supplement Yahweh's blessing, which is completely sufficient.

contrast between the righteous and the wicked with their respective fates. The words *ṣaddîq* and/or *rāšā'* occur in seven of them (vv. 24, 25, 27, 28, 30, 31, 32), while in other verses equivalent terms are used. Only v. 26 is an exception.

The group seems to have incorporated smaller groups. Verses 27-28 and 29-30 have already been identified as pairs formed by the addition of Yahweh proverbs, which now set the tone for the larger group. The two Yahweh proverbs stand in a context of verses which speak in different ways of the positive rewards which will be given to the righteous (vv. 24, 25, 28) and of the destruction of the wicked. To these they add long life for those who fear Yahweh (v. 27) and complete protection for the righteous (v. 29). Thus like vv. 3 and 22 they make it clear that it is Yahweh who is in control of the retribution referred to in the other verses. It has been suggested, however, that vv. 31-32, with their specific concern about the *speech* of righteous and wicked, may have been subsequent additions to the group, whose conclusion may earlier have been the general statements of v. 30. If this is the case, it is possible that vv. 1-30 have been made to constitute a large loosely connected group with an introduction in vv. 1-5 and a conclusion in v. 30.

Chapter 11

> Hermisson 2-14, 17-21, 23-31
> Plöger 3-6 (8), 9-15, 18-21, 23-31
> Krispenz 3-6, 17-21
> Meinhold 1-2, 3-8, 9-15, 16-22, 23-27, 28-30

This chapter does not appear to constitute a unity; and only some parts of it can reasonably be seen as forming distinct groups.

Verse 1 is completely unrelated to the verses which follow. It does rather have a tenuous link with 10.32 in that the two verses have in common the word *rāṣôn*, 'delight, acceptance'. But this is no more than a verbal link: there is no thematic connection. At any rate, 11.1 cannot be considered a pivotal verse between two groups. Verse 2 also appears to be an isolated verse.

Verses 3-11, however, are thematically closely related; they are also all, with the exception of v. 7, in antithetical parallelism. All these verses are statements about the respective fates of the righteous and the wicked: *ṣaddîq/ṣ^edāqâ* occur in vv. 4, 5, 6, 8, 9 and 10 and *rāšā'* in vv. 5, 7, 8, 10 and 11. There are also similarities between individual verses here. Verses 3a, 5a and 6a have a similar form. Verses 10 and 11, as has been observed above, form a pair.

But this group may extend to v. 14. Verses 9-13 turn from statements about individual moral behaviour and its effects on the persons concerned to its effects on the community (neighbour, city); v. 14 also speaks about the fate of a whole people (*'am*). Verses 3-14 should probably, therefore, be seen as a single group, but one which has been formed out of smaller ones.

Verses 15 and 16 appear to be isolated proverbs. But there is a clear thematic unity in vv. 17-21, all of which are in antithetical parallelism. They are all concerned with the righteous and the wicked; in vv. 17-19 there is a progressive heightening of the benefits promised to the former and the fates awaiting the latter, ending with the statement in v. 19 that these are not merely benefit and harm, not merely reward and disappointment, but life and death. These fates are then accounted for theologically by the Yahweh proverbs in v. 20 and its accompanying verse, 21. This group has no clear relationship to its immediate context. Krispenz pointed out that vv. 16 and 22 deal with the same topic—a pair of comments on different types of woman—but since the intervening verses make no mention of this or of related topics, it can hardly be maintained that vv. 16 and 22 mark the beginning and end of a distinct group.

In the second half of the chapter, vv. 24-26 clearly form a small group. Their theme is generosity as contrasted with miserliness. In vv. 25 and 26 there is a deliberate play on the meanings of the word *bᵉrākâ* which occurs in both: in v. 25 the *nepeš-bᵉrākâ* is the generous person who *gives* 'blessings' to the poor; v. 26 concerns the person who will *receive* a blessing. Otherwise there is no sign of a unified collection here. Both vv. 27 and 30 are obscure.

Chapter 12

The structure of this chapter has already been discussed in general terms.[28] Although it may have constituted a single instruction at a fairly late stage (v. 28, though the text is uncertain,[29] may have

---

28. See pp. 86, 87 above.

29. The second line reads, literally, 'and the way of a path not (*'al-*) death'. Most commentators read *'el* for *'al*, so '*to* death'. *nᵉtîbâ*, 'path', has been thought to be an

marked its conclusion; the following verse, 13.1, certainly marks a new beginning), it is clearly composite. The Yahweh proverb v. 2 offers a theological interpretation of the recommendation to accept discipline in v. 1, which is also applicable to the verses which follow. Verses 2-7, with the exception of v. 4, are thematically related, being concerned with the contrast between righteous and wicked. Within this section, vv. 5-7 mark a development of the theme, speaking respectively of the thoughts (v. 5), the words and actions (v. 6) and the respective fates (v. 7) of such persons. Verse 4, about the admirable and the shameful wife, differs from its context in its specificity. Hermisson suggested that it may be linked with vv. 3 and 5 by paronomasia (*bal*, 'not', v. 3; *ba'lāh*, 'her husband', v. 4: *mᵉbîšâ*, 'brings shame', v. 4; *mahšᵉbôt*, 'thoughts', v. 5). The verse may, however, be intrusive: vv. 3 and 5 have a common link in *reša'* (v. 3) and *rᵉšā'îm* (v. 5). Verses 8-13 pursue the theme of righteous and wicked further with specific examples, vv. 9-11 being concerned particularly with the daily life of the small farmer. The text of v. 12 is uncertain,[30] but vv. 12-14 continue the theme of righteous and wicked, now again in general terms.

Verse 15, which begins the second half of the chapter, strongly resembles v. 1; v. 16 may be seen as a concrete illustration of the assertion which it makes. Both are concerned with the fool (*'ᵉwîl*) and the wise or prudent; the respective consequences of listening and ignoring advice (v. 15) are seen in action in v. 16. The whole of vv. 15-23 is concerned with speech—righteous and wicked, wise and foolish—a topic already broached in vv. 13 and 14. That is to say, vv. 15-23 are concerned with one aspect of the theme of vv. 8-13.

There are also verbal links between some of the constituent verses of this section. *'ᵉwîl* occurs in vv. 15 and 16; *lāšôn*, 'tongue', in vv. 18 and 19. There is also a similarity between vv. 16 and 23, both thematic and verbal; *kōseh qālôn*, 'conceals humiliation', in v. 16 is matched by *kōseh dā'at*, 'conceals knowledge', in v. 23. This suggests the existence of a sub-group here. Verses 17, 19 and 22 are all similar

error for *rᵉšā'îm*, 'wicked' (cf. v. 26); alternatively, 'the wicked' may have been omitted, the line having originally read 'but the way of the wicked is a path to death'; but this would make an unusually long line. Other suggestions have been made.

30. The first line of v. 12 is unintelligible. In the second line *yittēn*, 'will give' may be an error for *'êtān*, '(is) enduring'; cf. LXX.

in content. The Yahweh proverb in v. 22 sets the theological tone for the group. Verses 24-28, however, manifest no consistency of form or theme.

Chapter 13

> Hermisson 1-6, 7-11, 12-19, 20-25 (+ 14.1)
> Meinhold 1-11, 12-19, 20-25

As has already been observed, this chapter is dominated by the theme of the need to accept instruction and discipline: this theme occurs, with characteristic vocabulary, in vv. 1, 13, 14, 18, 20 and 24, and is also echoed in vv. 10, 15 and 16. Whatever smaller groups may have been incorporated into it, the chapter now constitutes a single instruction though of a fairly loose kind. Verses 1 and 24 with their specific references to the education of children mark its beginning and end; it may be noted that Plöger, in view of the thematic connection between vv. 23 and 25, considers that v. 24 may once have stood at the end of the chapter. It is notable that the chapter did not undergo a 'theological' recension: unlike the other chapters of the collection (10.1–22.16) it contains no reference to God.

Although vv. 13 and 14 could be seen as introductory to a new instruction and despite the views of Hermisson and Plöger, who postulate a break between vv. 11 and 12, a case can be made for vv. 12-19 as constituting the core of the chapter in its final form, in view of the frequency of their references to the teaching of the wise (vv. 13-16, 18). These verses also have a chiastic arrangement. Verses 12 and 19 express similar thoughts; vv. 13 and 18 are equally concerned with the acceptance or rejection of instruction. The connection between vv. 14 and 17 is less clear. Verse 14 is similar to v. 13; v. 17 may be a particular example of the stress on prudence in v. 16. Verses 14 and 15, at the centre of the group, have similar themes: v. 15 speaks of the 'good sense' (*śēkel-ṭôb*) which results from heeding the 'teaching of the wise' in v. 14.

There are also other links, both thematic and verbal, between adjacent verses. Verses 2 and 3 pick up the thought of v. 1 on paying heed to the father's instruction by stressing the importance of right speech in general and the need to exercise control over one's words. Verses 2-4 are also linked by the occurrence of the word *nepeš* ('desire' or 'appetite' in vv. 2 and 4; 'life' in v. 3). Verse 5 reverts to the theme of speech, describing the characters of the righteous and the wicked; v. 6 comments on this, specifying their respective fates. Verses 7 and 8 are both concerned with wealth and poverty, though their interpretation is somewhat obscure. Verse 11 may be intended to be a concrete instance of the consequences of taking or not taking advice referred to in v. 10; there is evidently a close connection between v. 10 and vv. 12-19.

There are also internal links within vv. 20-25. Verse 20 is a further recommendation to associate with the wise; v. 21 interprets this in terms of sinners (*ḥaṭṭā'îm*) and righteous, the former word being picked up by 'sinner' (*ḥôṭē'*) in v. 22, which provides concrete examples. Verse 23 is unfortunately obscure,[31] but its reference to the poor probably suggested some relationship with v. 22 which is concerned with wealth. Verse 25 is probably related to vv. 22 and 23: like the former, it speaks of destitution for the wicked and prosperity for the righteous.

Chapter 14

>   Hermisson 1, 2-14, 15-22 (23), 24-35
>   Plöger 10-14, 20-24, 26-27, 28-35
>   Meinhold 1-3, 5-9, 10-14, 15-18, 19-24, 25-27, 28-35

Verse 1 of this chapter (accepting the deletion of *nāšîm*, 'women', and the emendation to *ḥokmôt*, 'Wisdom', as probably correct)[32] can hardly be understood in any other way than as an introduction to an instruction. Although it differs in form from 10.1, 12.1 and 13.1, it clearly belongs to the same literary tradition as 9.1, the first lines of the two verses being identical. Prov. 9.1 introduces the poem of ch. 9, in which the positive and wholesome attractions of the personified Wisdom and the destructive and death-dealing attractions of Folly are dramatically set out in detail. In 14.1 also the alternatives are briefly set out: as in ch. 9, a choice is offered to the person or pupil undergoing instruction; and the verses which follow, especially in the

---

31. The main problem concerns the first line, which states that the land owned by the poor (*rā'šîm*) produces plenty of food. This is contrary to what is said elsewhere about the 'poor', that is, those who are destitute. Various emendations have been proposed, e.g. *yᵉšārîm*, 'the righteous'; but no consensus has been reached.

32. With these emendations the first line becomes identical with 9.1a. MT has 'The wisest (plural) of women has (singular) built her house'.

first half of the chapter, are to be seen as illustrating the choice to be made and its consequences with concrete examples.

The point at which this instruction ends is not clear. On the one hand, v. 12 would make a suitable conclusion, as it may be said to sum up much of the foregoing verses by a final reference to the choice offered in v. 1: it implies that to trust one's own desires or one's own unaided judgment rather than accepting the guidance of Wisdom leads to death. On the other hand, there is a verbal link between vv. 12 and 13 in the word *'ah*^{a}*rît*, 'end', which occurs in both. This, however, could be a device to link one group with another; and it is possible that vv. 13ff. were added subsequently to the previous group. Verse 24, however, may also constitute the conclusion of a longer instruction beginning with v. 1, with which it also has strong affinities; or, as a further possibility, vv. 26-27, which as a pair of Yahweh proverbs may be said to end the instruction on a theological note.

No single theme is treated in this chapter, and many verses appear to be unrelated to those adjacent to them, although there are also some pairs or short groups connected either thematically or verbally. To some extent a chain of verbal links can be traced.

Verses 1-3 form a thematic group with v. 2, a Yahweh proverb, at its centre. Verse 3 gives an example of the kind of choice offered in v. 1, while v. 2 interprets it in terms of loyalty or disloyalty towards Yahweh. Verse 4 is probably intended to give a further example of wisdom and folly in terms of sensible and foolish farming methods. Verse 5, a condemnation of malicious lying, may be said to exemplify v. 2. Verses 6-8 resume the theme of wisdom and folly; and v. 9, also concerned with folly, is linked to v. 8 by the occurrence of *'iwwelet* in v. 8 and *'*^{e}*wīlîm* in v. 9. But the text of v. 9 is uncertain.[33] Verse 10 appears isolated, though a similar sentiment concerning the gladness of the heart (*lēb*) is found in v. 13. The reference to the upright (*y*^{e}*šārîm*) in v. 9 is picked up in both vv. 11 and 12, although in v. 12 *yāšār* is used in a quite different context: that verse refers to the person who is mistaken in thinking that the conduct which he wishes to pursue is 'right'. Verse 11 could be a comment on this. The house of the wicked (*bêt r*^{e}*šā'îm*) in v. 11 may

---

33. MT has 'guilt scorns fools, and between the righteous is favour'. The text is evidently corrupt; but no convincing emendation has been proposed.

be intended to recall the house built by Wisdom in v. 1; if so, there is a kind of parallel with the contrast between the 'houses' of Wisdom and of Folly in ch. 9.

Verses 12 and 13, as has already been remarked, are linked by the occurrence of the word *'aḥᵃrît*, 'end'. Similarly, vv. 13 and 14, though unconnected thematically, have *lēb*, 'heart', in common. Verses 15-18 form a distinct group concerned with the wise and fools, employing identical or synonymous vocabulary: vv. 15 and 18 both have *petî/pᵉtā'yim*, 'simple', and *'ārûm*, 'prudent'; *'iwwelet*, 'folly', occurs in vv. 17 and 18; *ḥākām*, 'wise', and *kᵉsîl*, 'fool', in v. 16. There are instances of paronomasia in vv. 19 and 20. Verses 20 and 21 (and probably also v. 19) are related thematically, and also by their similar beginnings: *gam-lᵉrē'ēhû*, 'even by his neighbour', v. 20; *bāz-lᵉrē'ēhû*, 'he who despises his neighbour', v. 21. Verse 22 could be a general comment on the wickedness portrayed in vv. 20 and 21. Verses 23 and 24 both refer to wealth and prosperity (*môtār*, 'profit', v. 23; *'ōšer*, 'wealth', v. 24), v. 23 offering a specific example of the more general statement of v. 24. Verses 26 and 27 may be intended as a comment on the statement about true and false witness in v. 25; but they may also constitute an emphatic conclusion to the foregoing verses, summing them up in the phrase 'the fear of Yahweh'.

Verses 28-35 appear to constitute a separate group, though this may continue as far as 15.4. Verses 28 and 35 are royal proverbs. Verse 28 points out that kings must behave so as to retain the loyalty of their subjects, while v. 35 refers to the king's duty, and ability, to reward his 'servants' as they deserve. Several of the intervening verses, although individually generally applicable, could well also be applied to kings. Verses 29-30 recommend a cool temper and a healthy (or relaxed) mind (*lēb marpē'*) in dealing with others. Verse 32 could be seen as a recommendation to kings to rule justly (compare 31.9). Verse 33 speaks of wisdom, which is constantly stated to be a requirement for kings, and verse 34 echoes the national note of v. 28 (*gôy, lᵉ'ōm*, 'people', v. 34: *'ām, gôy*, v. 28). The two verses together speak of the reciprocal relationship of king and people. Central to vv. 28-35 is v. 31, which is closely related to v. 32 but judges human relationships (which by implication include those of the king) by the criterion that all are God's creatures ('his Maker').

Verses 28-35, then, may have been placed here deliberately in close proximity to the central section of these chapters (16.1-15) which concerns the relationship between kings and Yahweh. This would be particularly true if v. 27, in addition to being the conclusion of the previous group, were a pivotal verse introducing the group which follows: the fear of Yahweh as the only route to 'life' is as appropriate to the behaviour of kings as to anything in the previous verses.

There is also a possible extension of vv. 28-35 into ch. 15, probably ending with the Yahweh proverb, 15.3. Prov. 15.1 and 2 can certainly be seen as related to 14.35: the king has God-given ability to discern good and evil (v. 35) and the capacity to create harmony by gentle and wise speech (15.1, 2); but his activities are ultimately subject to the teaching and judgment of Yahweh, from whom nothing can be hidden. There may also be a link with 15.4.

Proverbs 15.5-33

> Hermisson 8-11, 12-15, 20-23, 25-29, 30-33
> Hildebrandt 8-9, 11-12
> Krispenz 11-17, 25-33
> Meinhold 5-12, 13-19, 20-24, 25-33

This chapter is characterized by its theological tone. Of its thirty-three verses, nine are Yahweh proverbs (vv. 3, 8, 9, 11, 16, 25, 26, 29, 33). In the final nine verses (25-33) the proportion of Yahweh verses rises to almost half (vv. 25, 26, 29, 33).

Verse 5, on the importance of a son's paying attention to his father's instruction (*mûsar 'ābîw*) and heeding admonition (*tôkaḥat*), together with v. 7 on wise and foolish speech, appears to mark the commencement of an instruction. (The intervening v. 6, which promises wealth to the righteous and trouble for the wicked, is not closely related thematically to vv. 5 and 7; but it may have been placed here to express an editorial concern to make the point that true wisdom is consonant with righteousness and folly with wickedness; cf. vv. 8-11.) There follow three groups of proverbs which were probably once distinct but have been assembled to form a longer group: vv. 8-11, 12-17, 20-33. Each contains one or more Yahweh proverbs.

Verses 8-11, of which all except one (v. 10) are Yahweh proverbs, constitute an elaborate reinterpretation of 'wise' and 'fools' in moral terms as closely linked to 'righteous' and 'wicked' and as coming under the judgment of Yahweh (compare v. 6). This group as a whole appears to have developed from the non-Yahweh proverb v. 10. This verse speaks of 'forsaking the way'; but this, in the original intention of the phrase, referred to the 'way' of wisdom and discipline: that is, to the behaviour taught by the human teacher in v. 5. In v. 9 this 'way' is reinterpreted as the pursuit of righteousness; the 'way' has in v. 9 become the antithesis (though a different word is used) of the 'way of the wicked' which is abomination to Yahweh.

This is a tightly knit group. Verses 8 and 9 both speak of what is abomination to Yahweh and to what is pleasing to him; the first lines of these verses speak respectively of the sacrifice and the 'way' of the wicked, this being the only detail in which these lines differ, though the elements appear in a different order. Verses 10 and 11 are linked by references to death (death/Sheol). Thematically v. 11, the final verse of the group, provides an explanation of the condemnatory sentences of the previous verses: it is Yahweh who controls death; and the deeds of the wicked will not pass unnoticed by him who sees into the hearts of men. There is a development of thought from outward religious observance (sacrifice, prayer) in v. 8 to a more general field of behaviour ('way', vv. 9 and 10) and then to judgment.

Verses 12-17 may appear to have no single theme; one theme is nevertheless prominent: of these six verses, four (vv. 13, 15-17) are concerned with happiness or cheerfulness. Verse 13 is a 'psychological' observation; the first line observes that a cheerful heart (*lēb śāmēaḥ*) manifests itself in the face. Verse 15 picks up this topic, referring to 'happiness of heart' (*ṭôb-lēb*) as a 'continual feast' which can be enjoyed even by the hard-pressed poor. This notion is then carried further in vv. 16 and 17 in two comparative proverbs ('Better is...than...'), of which v. 16, a Yahweh proverb, is clearly a comment on v. 17: the latter verse, which picks up the topic of eating a meal from v. 15, asserts that a simple meal eaten in an atmosphere of love (*'ahªbâ*) gives more pleasure than a sumptuous dinner eaten in an atmosphere of hatred, while v. 16 expresses a similar thought but complements this 'love' with the fear of Yahweh, the source of such domestic harmony. These assertions are interspersed with verses (12 and 14) which stress the importance of accepting the teaching of the wise, which v. 16, by implication, interprets as equivalent to the fear of Yahweh.

There are also verbal links between verses in this group. The word *lēb*, 'heart', already found in v. 11, occurs also in vv. 13, 14 and 15. Verses 12-14 all begin with the same letter and with a monosyllable (*lō'*, *lēb*, *lēb*); vv. 15-17 all contain the word *ṭôb* ('happy, better'). Verses 16 and 17 are formally very similar. There is a general concern with human feelings in this group. The two verses which follow it, however (vv. 18 and 19) appear to be unconnected with it, unless the 'wrath' of v. 19 (*ḥēmâ*) may be said to pick up the reference to hatred in v. 17.

Verse 20 has close affinities with 10.1 and 13.1, each of which stands at the head of a distinct group of proverbs. Its first line is identical with 10.1a (cf. also 13.1a), and the mention of the mother alongside the father is also common to both verses. The purpose of the verse is clearly to stress the importance for the young of becoming wise through heeding their parents' teaching; and the verses which follow (21-24) elaborate on this theme: v. 21 praises the conduct of the man of understanding (*'îš tᵉbûnâ*) as against that of the person without sense; v. 22 stresses the importance of taking advice before acting; v. 23 speaks of the importance of the skill of appropriate speech. Verse 24 concludes by pointing out the consequences of making or refusing advice: life and death. All this general advice suggests that these verses are the introductory section of an instruction.

After an interval of several verses, vv. 31-33 revert to the initial theme. Verse 31 speaks of the wise (*ḥᵃkāmîm*) who pay attention to the admonition that leads to life (*tôkaḥat ḥayyîm*); v. 32 picks up the phrase 'heeds admonition' (*sômēa' tôkaḥat*) from v. 31 and contrasts this with ignoring instruction (*mûsār*). Finally v. 33, a Yahweh proverb, interprets the instruction in wisdom (*mûsar ḥokmâ*) recommended in the previous verses as equivalent to the fear of Yahweh. These verses could be seen as the opening verses of a new instruction; but it is more probable that, on the contrary, they mark the *end* of one. One of the indications of this is that they are linked verbally to what precedes by a remarkable series of references to the body or to its organs of perception: heart, mouth (v. 28); 'hears' (v. 29); eye, heart, what one hears (*šᵉmû'â*), body (*'eṣem*, v. 30); 'the ear that hears' (*'ōzen šōma'at*, v. 31); *nepeš*, 'self', i.e. the whole person, 'hears', heart (v. 32).

Between these two clearly related groups of verses (20-24 and 31-33) are sandwiched a series of verses concerned with righteousness and wickedness. This group is dominated by Yahweh proverbs (vv. 25, 26, 29), making up one half of the total. Verses 25 and 27 both refer to specific acts of wickedness. In both cases the house (*bayit*) of the wicked persons will be destroyed. Verse 25 states that this punishment will be inflicted by Yahweh himself, and this is clearly implied by v. 27 in its present position, especially as the intervening v. 26 expresses Yahweh's abhorrence of all wickedness. Again in v. 29 the statement that Yahweh will hear the prayer of the righteous but will not listen to (literally, 'is far from') the wicked is probably a comment on v. 28, which contrasts the flow of words from the wicked with the considered speech of the righteous.

There are thus three consecutive groups of verses in vv. 20-33: a series contrasting the righteous and the wicked with a heavy emphasis on the role of Yahweh as judge and distributor of rewards and punishment has been placed between two passages whose theme is the need to receive instruction and to acquire wisdom, which is also identified with the fear of Yahweh. There is reason to suppose that these three passages have been combined to form a single instruction. There is more than a slight similarity here to the structure of the instructions in chs. 1–9. Those instructions also begin with an appeal to heed the teacher's instruction and to receive wisdom, also speaking of the rewards which will be given to those who do so. This introductory section is followed, as here in vv. 25-29, by a concrete admonition or admonitions, which may be quite brief (compare, e.g., 2.16-19). There may follow a concluding section of general remarks about the respective fates of the righteous and wicked or of the wise and foolish (so, for example, 2.20-22), and this is paralleled here in vv. 30-33. Verses 20-33, then, constitute a complete instruction; however, the two halves of the chapter (from v. 5) have strong affinities, and in their present arrangement vv. 5-33 probably form a single instruction of chiastic form, vv. 31-33 corresponding to vv. 5ff.

Chapter 16

> Plöger 1-9, 10-15, 17-20, 21-24, 27-30
> Krispenz 1-9, 10-16

Some aspects of this chapter, especially of vv. 1-15, have already been discussed above.[34] Although it contains several originally distinct

34. Pp. 87-91.

groups, the strong similarity of its opening and closing verses (1 and 33) suggest that these have been combined to form a single unit.

Prov. 15.33, which marks the conclusion of ch. 15, is probably a pivotal verse joining these two chapters together: its first line is a general statement identifying wisdom with the fear of Yahweh which, though with variations (cf. 1.7 and 9.10), may have been a common-place or slogan of 'theological' wisdom literature. It is thus equally appropriate either at the beginning or the end of a piece of wisdom literature. The second line, which asserts that humility is more estimable than popular esteem or material prosperity (*kābôd*), also expresses a notion particularly appropriate to the theme of the verses which follow.

Verses 1-9 and 10-15, though no doubt originally separate entities, have been deliberately combined. This can be observed on the structural level: there is an alternation at the point where the two passages join between their respective topics: vv. 9 and 11 are Yahweh proverbs, while vv. 10 and 12 are royal proverbs, so that the two passages intertwine. The reason for this juxtaposition has been discussed above, but needs further detailed explanation in view of the central position of this pericope in the book. The two topics which are here given such prominence—Yahweh and the king—are topics which not only occur frequently in Proverbs but are also of central importance in the Old Testament as a whole.

The individual proverbs in these verses have been selected and arranged to create a unit which expresses an editorial view of the mutual relationship between Yahweh and the king. The first part, vv. 1-9, presents a comprehensive picture of Yahweh as in total control of human affairs. Verses 1 and 9 form a framework within which the intervening proverbs expound and illustrate this conviction. Yahweh tests and understands human motives (v. 2); human plans will be successful only if they are submitted to him (v. 3); he has, and he will carry out, a specific purpose for everything that he has created (v. 4); he will punish all human arrogance, which is a derogation of his prerogative (v. 5); consequently, obedience to his moral demands is the only guarantee of safety, and can cancel out previous sin (v. 6); the possession of his favour will bring security from the hostile intentions of enemies (v. 7). Verse 8 does not mention Yahweh and is less clearly related to its context; it may have been intended to illustrate the 'ways to please Yahweh' of v. 7.

What is said in these verses about Yahweh and his ways with people is also, of course, applicable to his relationship with kings as human beings, and in some cases particularly so. Thus royal policies need to be submitted to Yahweh if they are to succeed (cf. vv. 1, 3, 9); the motives of kings, like those of other people, are subject to Yahweh's scrutiny (cf. v. 2); kings are especially prone to the sin of pride, which is particularly abhorrent to Yahweh (cf. v. 5); they frequently have enemies from whose attacks Yahweh can save them if he approves of their conduct (cf. v. 7); and they are as much subject to Yahweh's religious and moral demands as anyone else (cf. v. 6).

In the royal proverbs, vv. 10-15, this point, that what is required of kings is the same as what is required of ordinary men and women, in even more clearly brought out. The king's throne remains secure only in so far as it is founded on righteousness (v. 12; cf.vv. 4 and 6), and it is the king's duty to promote and favour those who speak the truth (v. 13; cf. vv. 2 and 8). Verse 11, on commercial honesty, although it does not mention the king directly, also probably belongs here because it was one of the king's duties to set and maintain a standard of weights and measures, of which Yahweh himself was the guardian (cf. v. 2, which presents Yahweh as one who tests or weighs). These verses, then, speak of the king as subject to Yahweh and under his moral guidance (cf. vv. 2, 3 and 9).

But there is another fundamental aspect of monarchy which is also brought out here: the king is Yahweh's representative on earth, and has received from him powers which properly belong to him, so that a limited analogy can be made in this sense between the king and God. The king possesses divine powers of judgment (v. 10; cf. vv. 2 and 7, and see also 2 Sam. 14.17 and 1 Kgs 3 for the notion); and he possesses the power of life and death over his subjects (vv. 14, 15; cf. vv. 4 and 5). In 16.1-15, then, an editor has skilfully assembled two collections of proverbs, the one on Yahweh and the other on the nature of kingship, so that one reflects and illustrates the other.

Further, if 15.33 is, as has been suggested above, a pivotal verse, its equation of wisdom with the fear of Yahweh enables the whole of what is said in 16.1-15, about Yahweh and kings and the relationship between them, to be seen as an aspect of the wisdom with which 15.20-33 is concerned.

Verse 16 recommends the acquisition of wisdom, extolling its value in the same terms as are found in some of the instructions in chs. 1–9

('Get wisdom' and '[Get] understanding' occur also in 4.5; 'better than gold...silver' is paralleled in 3.14), and may thus be seen as the beginning of an instruction, although it is also related to the previous group. Its theme and vocabulary are echoed in vv. 21-23 and perhaps also in v. 20, a Yahweh proverb which associates instruction (here *dābār*, 'word') with trust in Yahweh, promising success to those who acquire it. There is thus good reason to see vv. 16-23 as a distinct instruction. Verse 17 is a general recommendation to avoid evil; vv. 18 and 19 advocate humility, a quality needful to those who set themselves to submit to instruction. There are also a number of verbal affinities in this group. Words for 'wise' and 'wisdom' occur in vv. 16, 21, 22, 23; vv. 18 and 19 both contain the word *rûah*, 'spirit', and vv. 21 and 23 *lēb*, 'heart'. *tôb*, 'better, prosper' (literally, 'find good', v. 20), occurs in vv. 16, 19 and 20. Verses 21 and 23 both contain the phrase *yōsîp leqah*, 'increases persuasiveness'. The Yahweh proverb v. 20 is central to this group, performing its familiar function of identifying wisdom (or instruction) with trust in him.

Verses 24-26 are loosely attached to the above group. Verse 24 has no real thematic connection with v. 23; it may have been appended to it because both verses refer to speech. There is also a verbal connection with v. 21. Verse 21 speaks of pleasant speech (*meteq śᵉpātayim*, literally 'sweetness of lips'), and v. 24 of pleasant words which are 'sweet to the palate' (*mātôq lannepeš*). Since the root *mtq*, 'sweetness', is extremely rare in biblical Hebrew (nine occurrences in all, of which three are in Proverbs), the connection between vv. 21 and 24 is unlikely to be accidental. There is a further point of similarity between vv. 23 and 26 in the occurrence of *pîhû*, 'his mouth'. However, vv. 24-26 have no common theme, though vv. 24 and 26 have the word *nepeš*, here 'palate', in common.

On the other hand, vv. 27-30 form a tightly knit group of verses about different types of person who disrupt community life. Such lists are found elsewhere in the book: compare especially 6.16-19. These verses also have a close formal similarity. This is particularly true of vv. 27-29, all of which begin with the same word *'îš*, 'a man of', which is the qualified by a noun denoting a particular kind of evil nature: worthlessness, deviousness (*tahpūkôt*), violence; and this is in turn followed by a verbal clause denoting a particular kind of wickedness. The second line in each case (these verses are in synonymous parallelism) describes the consequences. Verse 30 refers to another instance of wickedness, but with a slight formal difference: it begins with a participle ('He who...') and lacks the opening word *'îš*. With regard to possible links with vv. 16-23 it may be a coincidence that both vv. 23 and 27 contain the phrase 'on his lips' (*'al-śᵉpātâw*). On the other hand, the 'mouth' of v. 26 may have been the reason for the appending of this group of proverbs, which are mainly concerned in one way or another with speech.

If vv. 27-30 are intended as warnings about the evils which beset a young man, vv. 31 and 32 with their positive note may be intended to provide a counterbalance. Verse 31 is particularly appropriate in its present position: the goal presented here is a long life crowned at the end with honour for one who has avoided the pitfalls and lived a righteous life. Verse 32 is also appropriate in the context in asserting that the key to such a splendid career is self-control. Verse 33 may at first seem to be thematically unconnected with the preceding verses, but it provides a salutary reminder that the whole of human life is in the hands of Yahweh.

This final Yahweh proverb marks a return to the theme of the opening verses, especially of v. 1. This chiastic form may well suggest that there is a kind of unity to the whole chapter. Leaving aside vv. 24-26, which may have become attached to vv. 16-23 at a subsequent stage, it begins and ends with the theme of human status— including that of kings— as subordinate to Yahweh. After the initial verses it proceeds with the theme of the need for wisdom and instruction, continues with a list of dangers and temptations from evil persons encountered on the way, and concludes with a picture of the person who has resisted all the temptations and emerged into honoured old age—although still a human being whose subordinate status to Yahweh must be acknowledged.

Chapter 17

Plöger 27-28
Krispenz 26.1–18.8

In contrast with ch. 16 this chapter shows no sign of a comprehensive structure. There appear to be only a few short groupings here. One of these may be 16.33–17.3, 16.33 acting as a pivotal verse. This sequence of four verses consists of two Yahweh proverbs forming a framework to two proverbs (vv. 1 and 2) which have a certain thematic affinity. Verse 1 taken by itself is simply a variant of 15.16 and 17; but in its present context it shares with v. 2 the topic of a house divided. This is true, however, only of the second line of v. 1: the first line has no relationship at all with v. 2. But v. 2 offers a concrete example of the 'house full of strife' of v. 1b; the strife in question in this case is due to the promotion of a competent household slave to be the heir, and the demotion of the son of the house on account of his worthless behaviour. The two verses together constitute effective advice about acceptable and unacceptable conduct in family life. The two Yahweh proverbs, which assert Yahweh's control over human affairs (16.33) and his assessment of the human heart (v. 3) make the point that family life, like the other aspects of human existence and decision making, is ruled by an all-seeing and hidden God. There is also a certain similarity of topic with v. 6, which presents an *ideal* of family life; but vv. 4 and 5 hardly fit the theme, though some connection of v. 6 with vv. 1 and 2 may have been intended. Verses 7-10 appear to be unrelated both to one another and to their contexts.

Verses 11-13 all refer to calamities: the sending of the mysterious 'cruel messenger' (v. 11), the appearance of the dangerous she-bear (v. 12) and the evil (v. 13) which will not depart from the 'house' of the wicked, again perhaps an echo of vv. 1 and 2. Verse 14 with its reference to strife may also be an echo of v. 1, and v. 15 has a thematic affinity with v. 13. There may therefore have been some attempt to group together a number of verses on similar topics, but vv. 1-15 cannot be said to constitute a unified group.

Verses 21-25 may have been intended to form a short instruction. Verses 21 and 25 with their reference to the distress caused to parents by foolish children are closely related, and v. 24 similarly commends the acquisition of wisdom. Verse 22 picks up the 'no joy' of the unfortunate parent with its reference to a 'broken spirit'. Verse 23, however, speaks of wickedness rather than folly. Although the emphasis in vv. 21 and 25 is on the distress caused to parents, these verses may be intended as an appeal to the young to heed their parents' teaching, corresponding to the frequent admonitions in the instructions of chs. 1–9 to give satisfaction to parents and not to turn away from their advice.

Krispenz regards 17.26–18.8 as a distinct group (see below).

Chapter 18

> Plöger 4-8, 22-24
> Krispenz 17.26–18.8

Like ch. 17 this chapter contains no extended groups. Krispenz's argument that 17.26–18.8 forms a distinct group is not convincing, although there are connections between the final verses of ch. 17 (vv. 26-28). Verses 27 and 28 of that chapter are both concerned with knowing when to keep silent. In ch. 18 there are also some pairs and other very short groups. It has already been observed that vv. 1 and 2 are connected by the purely euphonic similarity between *yitgallā'* in v. 1 and *b^e hitgallôt* in v. 2. Verses 6-8 are linked by verbal repetition: *k^e sîl* ('fool'), 'lips' and 'mouth' all occur in both vv. 6 and 7, and there is another example of paronomasia in vv. 6 and 8 (*l^e mah^a lūmôt*, 'blows', v. 6; *k^e mitlah^a mîm*, 'delicious morsels', v. 8), here accompanied by a similarity of sense: all three verses (and also v. 4) are concerned with speech: vv. 6 and 7 both speak of the consequences of the speech of fools, and v. 8 also of the need to resist malicious gossip. The connections both verbal and thematic between vv. 10 and 11 have also been pointed out above.[35] Verse 12, with its reference to pride and humility, probably also belongs to this group.

Verse 15, on the importance of acquiring knowledge, may be, like other similar verses, the beginning of a new 'instruction'; but there is no indication of its extent. There is, however, a thematic connection between the four verses which follow (vv. 16-19). These can all be seen as concerned with disputes in the lawcourts. Verse 16 deals with bribery (without making a moral judgment); v. 17 with the need for sound judgment in deciding cases; v. 18 with the use of the lot in settling difficult cases; and v. 19, picking up the word *midwānîm/ midyānîm* ('disputes, quarrels') from v. 18, deprecates unnecessary litigation (we may note in this somewhat obscure verse the phrase *qiryat-'ōz*, repeated from v. 11; but the text here is very uncertain).[36]

Verses 20 and 21 may also be related to the previous verses: they are concerned with the power of speech. Verse 21 in particular may be a final comment on legal cases: there are some textual problems in

---

35. P. 77.

36. The first line, *'āh nipšā' miqqiryat-'ōz*, is certainly corrupt; no plausible emendation has been proposed.

these verses, but v. 21a is a clear statement that a person's life may depend on the spoken word. Verses 22-24 have different themes, but all refer to situations in family and community life, and may have been grouped together for this reason: marriage, care for the poor, and friendship.

Chapter 19

Plöger 18-23

This chapter contains such a large proportion of proverbs concerned with the importance of knowledge and instruction and/or the behaviour of children (vv. 2, 8, 13, 16, 18, 20, 25, 26, 27) that it must be understood as having been deliberately assembled for thematic reasons. However, although there are many links between individual verses including verses which are placed at some distance from one another, no large group can be discerned with certainty.

Verse 1a and 2 share the word *ṭôb*, 'good, better', but are not linked in any other way. Verses 2 and 3 are linked by images of life as a journey and of missing or losing one's way through folly; v. 3 extends the thought of v. 2, adding the comment that such persons, who have rejected the knowledge which was offered to them, blame Yahweh for their predicament.

Verses 4-7 are connected, partly verbally ('friend', *rēa'* or *rē'eh* occurs in vv. 6 and 7 and words for 'poor' in vv. 4 and 7), but also in theme: vv. 4b and 7 speak of the friendlessness of the poor, 4a and 6 of the popularity of the rich. Verse 5 strikes a warning note about the fate of those who use their wealth to procure perjured legal judgments. Verses 11 and 12 are both concerned with the topic of anger. Verse 11 may be intended to mitigate the statement in v. 12 about the king's anger by advocating an attitude of forbearance or forgiveness of offences. The reference to the quarrelling wife in v. 13b is countered by v. 14b with its praise of the intelligent wife who is a gift from Yahweh.

Verses 16-27 manifest a somewhat greater unity, but are probably the result of the combination of shorter groups. There is no progression of thought. While v. 27 is addressed by a father to a son and most of the individual proverbs conform to this stance, v. 18 is addressed not to a son but to a father. The fifteen verses 13-27 contain four Yahweh proverbs (vv. 14, 17, 21, 23) and five which advocate giving heed to instruction (vv. 16, 18, 20, 25, 27). There is a further reference to children in v. 26.

There are many links within these verses between individual proverbs. The statement in v. 16 about the importance of keeping the 'commandment' (*miṣwâ*), originally meaning parental instruction, has been glossed by v. 17, which gives a concrete example of such obedience and states that Yahweh will reward it, a statement later amplified in v. 23, which defines this reward as 'life' and as given to those who fear Yahweh. The admonition in v. 18 to discipline a child 'while there is hope' for him is closely related to v. 16 with its reference to the 'death' and 'life' which will be the destiny respectively of those who neglect or heed the father's commandment.

Verses 20 and 21 are linked by the occurrence in both of the word *'ēṣâ*, which in v. 20 refers to human advice but in v. 21 to Yahweh's 'purpose': although human advice may be an excellent thing, it is ultimately Yahweh who makes the decisions. Verse 22a, which states that loyalty (*ḥesed*) is especially desirable, may be linked to v. 23, which refers to obedience to Yahweh. Verses 19 and 24 appear to be isolated proverbs, but are perhaps to be seen as drawing attention to two faults of character which run contrary to all of the father's teaching: anger and sloth.

Chapter 20

Krispenz 5-13

No connection is discernible between vv. 1-4 or between them and what follows. Krispenz is correct in seeing vv. 5-12 as linked, but apart from a verbal connection between v. 12 and v. 13 in the common use of the word *'ayin*, 'eye', it is difficult to see v. 13 as belonging to this group. In vv. 5-12 every verse is concerned —though in a variety of ways—with the human mind and with the question how it may be possible to penetrate its secrets and discern human character. The unity of the group is strengthened by the particular links between consecutive verses.

Verses 5 and 6 are linked verbally by the occurrences of *'îš*, 'a man', and by expressions denoting inscrutability: 'deep water'; 'who can find...?' They are also thematically connected: v. 5 asserts that only a man of understanding can discover the secret intentions of another; v. 6 that it is very difficult, if not impossible, to assess the truth of another person's protestations of loyalty. Verse 7, however, acknowledges that righteous men do exist, and that they are blessed, together with their families. From v. 8 onwards the question who is able to distinguish the righteous from the wicked is again raised and discussed. Verse 8 suggests that it is the *king* who has special powers in this regard: he is a perceptive judge of wickedness. But v. 9, like v. 6 ('Who can find?'), expresses scepticism ('Who can say. . . ?') about the very possibility of human perfectibility. Verse 10, a verse with variants elsewhere in these proverbs (v. 23; cf. also 11.1; 16.11) has probably been placed here both as citing a common example of a fault (cf. 'evil', v. 8; 'sin', v. 9): commercial dishonesty, which easily passes unnoticed and can be committed by those who, as in v. 9, claim to be honest; but its more important function is to introduce Yahweh as the only one who—as is claimed for the king in v. 8—sets the norms of conduct and is able to discern and punish those who transgress them. It should also be noted that both this verse and v. 12 end with the same words, 'both of them' (*gam-šᵉnêhem*).

Verse 11 also is about discernment. It appears at first sight to contradict previous proverbs in the group by asserting that a person's character is easy to discern, even in children; but it may be intended only as a correction: it is only by people's *actions* that their character can be known ('By their fruits you shall know them'). This may also be the point of v. 12: Yahweh has given to everyone the organs of hearing and sight, so that they may be able to judge character by what they hear and see in the speech and actions of others. This makes a return to the thought of v. 5 about the 'man of understanding'.

Thus vv. 5 and 12 form the framework of the group. It cannot be said that in vv. 5-12 there is a continuity or progression of thought; rather, the question of the discernment of character is discussed from every angle; and in this sense there is a unity of thought here that cannot be accidental. This is a particularly clear example of a group of proverbs with thematic unity; and it is especially interesting in its obvious intention to provoke thought.

There is good reason to see 20.20–21.4 as a thematic group. These fifteen verses contain no less than seven Yahweh proverbs, all of which except v. 27 are arranged in triads: 20.22-24; 21.1-3. There are also three proverbs which refer to kings: 20.26, 28; 21.1. Prov. 21.1 is both a royal proverb and a Yahweh proverb. In these verses three relationships are discussed: (1) between Yahweh and people in general; (2) between Yahweh and the king; (3) between the king and his subjects. There are also verbal links, especially in the occurrences of *nēr* (*nīr*), 'lamp', vv. 20, 27; the contrasting 'curse' and 'bless' in vv. 20 and 21; the occurrence of *'ādām*, 'a man' (as against the more frequent *'îš*), in vv. 24, 25 and 27; the phrase *ḥadᵉrê-bāṭen*, 'innermost parts', in vv. 27 and 30; the words *lēb*, 'heart', in 21.1, 2 and 4 and *'ayin*, 'eye', in vv. 2 and 4.

Verses 20-25 are concerned with Yahweh's relationship with human beings. Verses 20 and 21 speak of the certainty that crimes will be punished; v. 22 stresses that it is Yahweh who will carry this out, and that private revenge is forbidden. Verse 23 gives an example of another crime which incurs Yahweh's abhorrence and so, by implication, his punishment of it. Verse 24, taken by itself, might seem to imply that human lives are entirely determined by Yahweh, but in this context it probably continues the thought of v. 23; everything should be left to him to deal with. Verse 25 follows this with a warning that, since Yahweh is in control, rash vows are foolish.

Prov. 20.26–21.4 are concerned, directly or by implication, with the king: his relationship with his subjects and his subordination to Yahweh. Verse 26, which speaks of the wise king who identifies and punishes the wicked (the meaning of the mysterious 'and drives the wheel over them' is irrelevant here)[37] is followed by v. 27 which makes it clear that human motives (including, by implication, those of the king) are subject to Yahweh's scrutiny, while v. 28 prescribes the king's duty to rule faithfully and justly. Verses 29 and 30 may at first seem to be thematically unrelated to the rest; but v. 29, which compares young and old men, could be seen as commending the wise king who has profited by his long experience. Verse 30 is obscure and probably corrupt;[38] it may refer to the possibility that punishment sometimes has a salutary effect.

Prov. 21.1-4 begins (v. 1) with a further statement that the king's

---

37. Literally, 'and causes a/the wheel to return over them'. This has been taken variously to refer to some kind of torture or to the 'wheel of fortune'. In view of the reference to winnowing in the first line, it is more likely that it refers to the wheel of a threshing-sledge (cf. Isa. 28.27-28).

38. In the first line the meaning of the word *tamrûq* (*kethib*; *tamrîq*, *qere*) is obscure. One possible meaning of the line would be 'Blows which wound cleanse away evil'.

mind (heart) is subject to Yahweh's control, and the remaining verses (2-4) are also particularly applicable to kings. Verse 2, with its assertion that Yahweh knows a person's heart better than does that person himself, v. 3 with its insistence on the need for righteousness and justice, and v. 4 with its warning against the sin of arrogance all fit into the pattern. The whole group (20.20–21.4) may be compared with 16.1-15 (see above).

Chapter 21

Krispenz 1-8
Plöger 30-31

Verses 1-4 have been considered under ch. 20. Krispenz, who sees 21.1-8 but not the previous verses as forming a distinct group, argues for a thematic connection of vv. 5-8 with vv. 1-4, but this is not clear. There are some verbal repetitions; but it is significant that after v. 3 there are no further references to Yahweh until the end of the chapter, and no further references to kings. The verbal links occur only in vv. 1-4; they are entirely lacking in vv. 5-6.

Nevertheless it is possible that at some point in the editorial process the whole chapter may have been invested with a kind of loose unity. This is suggested by the fact that it is framed by two proverbs which are strikingly similar in their theme. Both are concerned with kings; and they stress the fact that royal plans and activities are subject to the control of Yahweh. Verse 1 asserts that royal intentions (*lēb*, 'heart') may be overruled by Yahweh, while v. 31 (though the word *melek*, 'king', does not actually occur in this verse) speaks more concretely of royal preparations for war which are ineffective unless approved by Yahweh, because the outcome (*tešû'â*) will be as he decides. The theme is reminiscent of 16.1-9. Here, however, it appears from the adjacent verses (2, 30) that an a fortiori argumentation is intended: if even kings are subject to Yahweh's control, this is even more true of ordinary people. Verse 2, which is a variant of 16.2, speaks of 'hearts' (*libbôt*, plural) as subject to Yahweh's scrutiny and, presumably, judgment, while v. 30 asserts that there is no (*'ên*) human wisdom or understanding or planning (*'ēṣâ*) apart from Yahweh.

The remainder of the chapter consists of what at first appear to be quite miscellaneous proverbs; but the initial and final verses may be said to provide an interpretation of many of them: those which speak of human wisdom (vv. 11, 16, 20, 22) can now be seen in the light of the general principle that true wisdom can come only from Yahweh, and the numerous proverbs about the activities and fates of righteous and wicked (vv. 4, 6-8, 10, 12-15, 18, 21, 24, 26-29), which are introduced by the Yahweh proverb v. 3, can be seen in terms of judgment by Yahweh. The Yahweh proverbs in this chapter thus give a specifically religious tone to the whole chapter, even though a few verses on diligence and laziness (vv. 5, 25), love of pleasure (v. 17), and the nagging wife (twice!—vv. 9, 19) do not appear to fit the general scheme.

There are also some connections between individual verses of the chapter. Verses 5 and 6 are both concerned with the acquisition of wealth. Verse 6 is an extension of the thought of v. 5b: if the desire to get rich quickly leads in the end to poverty, the fate of those who acquire wealth by telling lies is worse: it is death. It has also been suggested that there may be a traditional sequence in the subjects treated in vv. 4-7: they strongly resemble the list of 'abominations' in 6.17-19, and in the same order: haughty eyes (v. 4), lying tongue (v. 6), violence (v. 7). There may also be a connection with v. 8, whose meaning is not entirely clear, but which seems to be a further comment on the characters of the righteous and the wicked.

Verses 10, 11 and 12 are also connected. Verses 10 and 12 taken together constitute an ironical comment on the wicked (*rāšā'*): in v. 10 the wicked person *desires* to do harm (*ra'*) to his neighbours; in v. 12 the 'righteous one' (*ṣaddîq*, thought by some commentators to refer to God) *gives* him what he desires for others: ruin (*ra'*). Verse 11 sees this ruin of the wicked as a source of instruction for both the simple and the wise. There is also a verbal link between vv. 11 and 12: *haśkîl*, 'instruction', v. 11; *maśkîl*, 'observes', v. 12.

Again, vv. 20, 21 and 22 are connected. Verse 20 states that the wise will have (or preserve) wealth, while v. 21 promises 'life' and honour (that is, prosperity) to the righteous. Verse 22 adds a further commendation of wisdom: its superiority over brute force. Verses 25 and 26 are concerned with greed (*ta'ᵃwâ*, 'desire', v. 25; *hit'awwâ*, 'covet', v. 26): it is fatal both to the lazy and the wicked; v. 26b adds that generosity rather than greed is the mark of the righteous. Verse 30 may be understood as a correction of v. 29b, especially if we read *yākîn*, 'establishes', for the difficult *yābîn*, 'understands': v. 29b may give the impression that the upright can 'establish his ways', that is, be successful, without divine assistance; v. 30 makes it clear that human wisdom is of no account beside the wisdom of Yahweh.

Proverbs 22.1-16

These sixteen verses, which conclude the major collection which begins with 10.1, contain four Yahweh proverbs (vv. 2, 4, 12, 14), six proverbs concerned with wealth and/or poverty (vv. 1, 2, 4, 7, 9, 16) and two on the training of children (vv. 6, 15), with a further verse on the importance of 'knowledge' (v. 12). The importance attached to the theme of wealth and poverty is shown by the fact that the group begins (vv. 1 and 2) and ends (v. 16) with proverbs on this subject. There is thus reason to see this as the principal theme of the chapter. The Yahweh proverbs vv. 2 and 4 make plain the concern of Yahweh with wealth, with a reminder that the poor are equally his concern as their creator (v. 2) and that wealth is given only to those who fear him (v. 4; 'humility' here may be a later addition to the verse).

Verse 1 introduces the subject by relativizing the importance of wealth: a good reputation in the community is more important—a piece of advice which would be especially relevant to a young man setting out on his career. Verse 2 is equally relevant to this advice. Verses 3 and 5 taken by themselves are not directly about wealth, but speak of the need to be wise (*'ārûm*, v. 3) and the consequences of being 'crooked' (*'iqqēš*, v. 5) in one's dealings, and this is interpreted in v. 4 in terms of fearing Yahweh, the only sure way to find wealth. Verse 6 picks up the reference to the 'way' (*derek*) of the crooked (v. 5) by speaking of the 'way' (*derek*) in which children must be trained, and which will be their guide throughout life. These six verses, then, hang together as instruction to the young.

Verse 7-9 also share the same topic. Verse 7 is a plain statement about the power conferred by wealth, a statement tempered by v. 8, which is a reminder that power must be accompanied by justice and mercy, and by v. 9, which speaks of the blessing that will be conferred on those who are generous to the poor.

Verse 10-12 may constitute a small group, though v. 11 is obscure and probably corrupt. (LXX has 'The Lord loves holy hearts' in the first line. The reference to the king in the Hebrew of the second line is dubious.) Verse 10 condemns those who make trouble for the community (*lēṣ*, 'scoffer); v. 12 speaks of the overthrow of the treacherous and states that Yahweh protects those who possess 'knowledge' (*da'at*).

Verse 13, a variant of 26.13, is quite unconnected with its context. Verse 15 resumes the theme of parental discipline already treated in v. 6 with a reference to youthful folly (*'iwwelet*); it is preceded by v. 14 which gives a concrete example of such folly, one to which young men are especially prone: seduction by 'strange women' (*zārôt*); this is the language, as well as the theme, of some of the instructions in chs. 1–9. Thus those who fail to respond to parental discipline will 'fall into a deep pit' as a consequence of Yahweh's anger. The meaning of v. 16 is not entirely clear,[39] but the first line clearly condemns the oppression of the poor, returning to the principal theme of the earlier verses.

Chapters 25–29
The separate collection comprising chs. 25–29, associated in 25.1 with the 'men of Hezekiah', differs from the earlier main collection (10.1–22.16) in various ways. It contains very few Yahweh proverbs: only six in all, of which three occur in ch. 29; chs. 26 and 27 have none at all. There is only one in ch. 25 and two in ch. 28. Chapters 25–27 also differ formally from chs. 28 and 29: the former collection is notable for the frequency of its cases of imagery, expressed in similes and metaphors, while the latter contains few examples of this.

Chapter 25

> Bryce 2-27
> Van Leeuwen 2-27
> Plöger 6-10, 11-12, 13-14, 16-22
> Krispenz 23-28
> Meinhold 11-22 (16-17, 18-20), 23-28

Two scholars, Bryce and Van Leeuwen, have argued that vv. 2-27 of this chapter constitute a single 'wisdom book' or 'proverb poem' divided into two parts (vv. 6-16, 17-27) preceded by an introduction (vv. 2-5). They see this originally distinct work as intended to give advice to courtiers or would-be courtiers. This view can hardly be sustained. It is true that vv. 1-7 all refer to kings; and since the

---

39. The two lines may have originally been unrelated, and it is possible that each is a fragment of a separate proverb part of which has been accidentally omitted.

heading in v. 1 states that the proverbs which follow were collected or edited for a king by his royal scribes, this may well account for the prominence given to kings in the six verses that follow. However, there are no further references to kings in the remainder of the chapter, although there is a reference to a 'ruler' (*qāṣîn*) in v. 15. But although some items in vv. 8-28 (especially vv. 11-15) could be interpreted as advice to courtiers, there is no particular reason to do so: they may be seen as of quite general reference; and the remaining verses of the chapter are concerned, like so many of the proverbs in the book, quite generally with such common matters as relations between neighbours. There is also no clearly educational reference.

In fact, it is not possible to discern a comprehensive structure in this chapter. Formally it is very varied: the main formal types are those of the statement in the form of a simile or comparison, and the admonition; the former is predominant. Examples of the latter are mainly longer than most of the proverbs found elsewhere (four lines rather than two), and are provided with motive clauses. The occurrences of the two types are not arranged according to any pattern; but from the point of view of composition it may be significant that in the main they form small groups of up to four verses: similes and comparisons (vv. 3-5, 11-15, 18-20, 24-28); admonitions (vv. 6-10, 16-17, 21-22). In some cases there are also thematic and/or verbal links between adjacent groups. But there is no comprehensive pattern, though the close verbal links pointed out by Bryce and Van Leeuwen between vv. 2-3 and v. 27b, which they regard as the conclusion of the 'wisdom book' or 'proverb poem', suggest that at one time vv. 2-27 may have been seen as an independent piece, even though not as an instruction to courtiers. This verbal link is striking: the mysterious v. 27b, which is probably corrupt and has no discernible link with the previous line (*wᵉḥēqer kᵉbōdām kābôd*, literally 'and the searching out of their glory is glory'), consists entirely of words which occur in vv. 2-3: v. 2 employs both *kābôd*, 'glory' (twice), and the infinitive *ḥᵃqōr*, 'to search out', and v. 3 employs the word *ḥēqer* as in v. 27b. The echo is unmistakable, though its purpose is quite unclear.

The word 'king' (or its plural) occurs in v. 1 and in each of the three subsequent units, vv. 2-3, 4-5, 6-7. In vv. 2-3, however, there is a thematic paradox concerning the nature of kings: in v. 2 the glory of kings is to search out things (while God conceals them, presumably even from kings), but on the other hand, according to v. 3 the minds of kings themselves are unsearchable, that is, hidden from other men. Verses 4-5 constitute a single comparison stressing the necessity of purging the wicked from the king's entourage. Verses 6-7b are an admonition which, if taken literally, appears to be addressed to the aspiring courtier; but it is the only such one in the chapter, and is intended to be a general application.[40] Verses 7c-8 and 9-10 are closely connected both verbally and thematically. They are both concerned with disputes (*rîb*), they both mention the neighbour (*rēa'*), and they both warn that an attempt to publicize a neighbour's faults may result in the public humiliation of the accuser.

Verses 11-15 (11-14 are all comparative proverbs) are, like vv. 7b-10, concerned with the right and wrong use of speech, but in different ways: the making of an appropriate choice of words (v. 11), the wise rebuke (v. 12), the message faithfully delivered (v. 13), the empty boast (v. 14), the persuasive speech (v. 15). Verses 11 and 12 are also connected by the choice of simile: wise speech is compared with a gold ornament. Verses 13 and 14 employ similes derived from climatic phenomena. Verses 16 and 17 have the same theme: the unfortunate results of excessive indulgence, v. 17 making its point in plain language while v. 16 makes it by means of a metaphor. Both proverbs employ the verb *śāba'*, 'to be sated, have too much', and the second lines of the two verses have the same syntactical structure as well as the same sense. (There also seems to be a link between v. 16 and v. 27a.) Verse 18 is also linked to this pair by the word 'neighbour' (*rēa'/rē'eh*), and v. 19 is thematically similar to v. 18 (false witness, treacherous person). The first lines of these two proverbs, and to some extent the second lines, have the same syntactical structure.

Verse 20 has almost certainly suffered some corruption in the form of a word or words added later,[41] but has the same syntactical arrangement as the preceding verses, and like them mentions something unpleasant as its point of comparison. Verses 21-22, a double proverb, is unconnected with its context. Verses 23 and 24 are both directed against anti-social behaviour. Verses 25 and 26 both use water imagery in their comparisons. Verses 27 (at least the first line)

---

40. See Plöger, *Sprüche*, p. 299.

41. The middle section, *ḥōmeṣ 'al-nāter*, 'vinegar on soda' (?), may be a fragment of another proverb: cf. LXX. But no solution has been found.

and 28 are both concerned with self-control, though the imagery employed is quite different.

Chapter 26

> Van Leeuwen 1-12, 13-16, 17-28
> Plöger 1-12, 13-16, 17-19, 20-28
> Krispenz 1-16, 17-22
> Meinhold 20-22, 23-25

This chapter is much more integrated than most of the chapters in this part of the book (25–29). There are three clear sections each having its own topic, and apart from the pivotal v. 12 they follow one another without intermingling. There is no direct reference to education, although there is a clear intention to instruct by offering many examples of persons whose characters are to be avoided. There is no reference to Yahweh and thus nothing to make plain the notion that it is he who passes judgment on the ills of society.

Verses 1-12, with one exception, deal explicitly with the fool: the word $k^e s\hat{\imath}l$ occurs in all these verses. But as Van Leeuwen recognized there is a further, related, topic here: the question as to what is, and what is not, appropriate or fitting in the life of a community. Verses 13-16 are all concerned with the lazy person, the *'āṣēl*. Verses 17-28 are a collection of proverbs about unpleasant people who disturb or harm the community. The whole chapter may thus be seen as a compendium of vignettes about the characters and behaviour of certain human types that may be met with in any community, classified under three headings. These may have originally been independent, but have clearly been combined because of their general theme. Within each section there are also sub-groups linked by both formal and verbal devices, of which, as in ch. 25, the simile or comparison is the most prominent (vv. 1-3, 5-11, 17-23).

Verse 1 defines the proper place of fools in society: they do not deserve to be given honorable status. Verse 2, the only verse in this section with no direct mention of the fool, may be seen as giving a further example of what is not fitting: just as it is unfitting to give a place of honour to fools, so it is equally unfitting to curse innocent individuals and so deprive them of their honourable position. Verse 3 then picks up v. 1 and states in very precise language what is fitting for fools: a rod for their back. Verses 4 and 5 pursue the question of how fools should be treated: what *is* fitting for them? There are two opposite ways of treating fools: to take them seriously or to ignore them. The exact repetition of the first lines of these two verses apart from the inclusion of the word 'not' in v. 4 presents the issue in a stark form and is intended to provoke serious reflection on the problem by stating a paradox.

The remaining verses of this group (6-12) are characterized by the use of bizarre imagery to stress the uselessness of fools and the fact that they are a danger to society. The duplication of a whole line in vv. 7b and 9b and of the thought of v. 1 about giving honour (*kābôd*) to a fool in v. 8 shows that vv. 1-12 were not composed as an integrated unit but were assembled editorially from separate proverbs. Verse 12, which repeats the reference in v. 5 to being 'wise in one's own eyes', is a transitional or pivotal verse. Unlike v. 5 it makes a distinction between such persons and fools and so anticipates the next section about the lazy, one of whose characteristics is precisely that they are exceptionally wise in their own eyes. Both types of person are seen as menaces to society.

Verses 13-16 form another obvious sub-group. Verses 13-15 are a collection of humorous sayings about the lazy, of which two found their way into other collections, v. 13 being a close variant of 22.13 and v. 15 of 19.24. Verse 16 completes and sums up the group with a general statement about the most dangerous characteristic of the lazy: their complacency.

Verses 17-28 are a collection of proverbs about persons who disturb the harmony of society, mainly by deceitful or malicious speech. They are linked by a distinctive vocabulary, of which the most frequent example is the root *śn'*, 'hate, enemy, enmity' (vv. 24, 26, 28); also *rîb*, 'quarrel' (vv. 17, 21); *nirgān*, 'slanderer' (vv. 20, 22). In some cases such keywords link adjacent verses: vv. 20 and 21, in which quarrelling is compared with fire, have three words in common: *'ēṣ*, 'wood', *'ēš*, 'fire', and *mādôn*, 'strife'; vv. 23 and 24 share *śepātayim*, 'lips'.

Within this group a distinction is made between two kinds of anti-social speech: while vv. 17-21 are concerned mainly with quarrels, vv. 22-26 deal with malicious, especially deceitful persons who dissimulate their hatred under a cloak of friendship. The final verses make a suitable conclusion to the group and to the chapter as a whole. Whereas in the immediately preceding verses these nefarious activities are merely described with no mention of the consequences to those who practise them, from v. 26b onwards the doctrine of retribution appears. Verse 26 states that the 'enemy's wickedness will be publicly exposed; v. 27 follows this with a general statement that the wicked will reap their reward; there is here a return to the notion of what is 'fitting' expressed in the first part of the chapter. This may also be the theme of v. 28, though there it is not clear whether the 'stumbling' or ruin envisaged in the second line refers to the fate of the liar or of his victim.

Chapter 27

Plöger 1-2, 5-10
Krispenz 3-9

Like ch. 26, this chapter contains no Yahweh proverb. It has no structural unity: but vv. 11-27 may once have constituted a loose compendium of parental teaching. In vv. 1-10 the topic of friendship plays a dominant, though not an exclusive, role.

Verses 1 and 2 are linked by the verb *hll*, 'boast' (*hithpael*, v. 1); 'praise' (*piel*, v. 2). They both deprecate self-assertive speech. Verses 3 and 4 both employ an a fortiori device. There may also be a deliberate progression here from *ka'as*, 'irritation, vexation', in v. 3 to the stronger words *ḥēmâ*, 'fury', *'ap*, 'anger', and *qin'â*, 'jealousy', in v. 4; but there is no real thematic connection between the two verses. Verses 5 and 6, however, are linked by the theme of friendship and the importance of plain speaking within this relationship; the root *'hb*, 'love' is common to both. There is no obvious connection between them and vv. 7 and 8, but the theme of friendship is renewed in vv. 9 and 10, if the word *rē'ēhû* is to be retained in the probably corrupt second line of v. 9.[42]

It is probably the admonition ('do not forsake...the friend of your father') in v. 10 which accounts for the placing of v. 11, which is an admonition from a father to a son. But v. 11, in which a father admonishes his son to acquire wisdom—that is, to heed his own teaching—clearly belongs to the same literary type as the introductory

---

42. A literal translation of this line would be 'and/but the sweetness of his friend from/than the advice of the soul (*nāpeš*)'. No satisfactory emendation of this obscure line has been proposed.

verses of the instructions of chs. 1–9. The proverbs which follow are on various topics mainly unrelated, but not inappropriate as parental advice; some of them are variants of proverbs found elsewhere in these chapters. The chapter ends with an extended admonition (vv. 23-27) about the importance of diligence and hard work. This is unusually long, and may well have been intended as an impressive conclusion to the instruction, to the chapter and even to this group of chapters (25–27; chs. 28–29, as is generally agreed, once formed a separate collection).

Although vv. 12-22 do not have a single common topic, there are connections between some of them. Verse 12 may be intended to add support to v. 11, as it draws a contrast between the respective fates of the prudent (*'ārûm*) and the simple (*petî*). Verses 12 and 13 may be linked by paronomasia (*'ārûm*; *'ārab*, 'give a pledge'). Verses 15 and 16 constitute a single proverb; v. 15 has a number of variants (19.13; 21.9, 19; 25.24); v. 16 is an elaboration of it.

Verses 18-22 are all reflections on human character. Verse 18 speaks of the reward for faithful, contented work, while v. 20, on the other hand, appears to doubt whether human beings are ever satisfied. The meaning of the interjacent v. 19 is not clear; but it is certainly also a reflection on human character. Verse 21 speaks of a way to test a person's character; v. 22, using a somewhat similar metaphor (the crushing of grain in a mortar, the smelting of metal in a furnace), asserts that the folly of fools is irradicable.

Chapter 28

Although this chapter also has no comprehensive structure, two things make it probable that it has been assembled to form an independent instruction, albeit of the looser kind. One is the frequency of occurrence of the word *tôrâ*, 'teaching' (four times; vv. 4 [twice], 7, 9) in the first nine verses, a word which occurs only twice (13.14; 29.18) in the rest of the sentence literature, and only thirteen times in the entire book; in all four instances it is governed by the verbs 'keep' (*šāmar*, *nāṣar*), 'heed' (*šāma'*) or 'do not forsake', precisely as in the instructions of chs. 1–9 (1.8; 3.1; 4.2; 6.20; 7.2), where the 'teaching' in question is that of the father or mother. The other is the fact that the majority of the proverbs in the chapter are of an ethical nature, dealing with the righteous and/or the wicked. Verse 7, which identifies one who keeps *tôrâ* with 'an intelligent son' (*bēn mēbîn*) and thus with wisdom, suggests that at least vv. 1-9, though not a formal introduction, are to be regarded as instructional material. There are two other explicit references in the chapter to wisdom: a warning against being wise (*ḥākām*) in one's own eyes (v. 11) and a commendation of those who 'walk in wisdom' (v. 26).

There are a number of other verbal and thematic connections between adjacent verses in a chapter which revolves around a few particular themes. In vv. 3-6 there are verbal echoes: *rāš*, 'poor', v. 3; *rāšā'*, 'wicked', v. 4; *an^ešê-rā'*, 'wicked men', v. 5; *rāš* again, v. 6. Verses 15 and 16 both speak of cruel and oppressive rulers. Verses 19-22 are all concerned in one way or another with wealth or the temptation of it and its consequences (*leḥem*, 'bread' occurs in vv. 19 and 21). Verses 25 and 26 are closely related, not only by the occurrence in both of *bôṭēaḥ*, 'he who trusts', but also in theme: the Yahweh proverb v. 25 makes it clear that trusting in Yahweh is connected with 'walking in wisdom' (v. 26). Both this and the other Yahweh proverb comment on the surrounding verses. The final verse (28) sums up the whole.

Chapter 29

This chapter has certain features in common with ch. 28, with respect both to the forms employed—especially the predominance of anti-thetical proverbs—and, to some extent, to its topics. It is noteworthy, for example, that one topic, which elsewhere occurs only rarely—that of the alternate rise to and fall from power of the righteous and the wicked respectively—occurs four times in these two chapters in variant forms, twice in each chapter (28.12, 28; 29.2, 16). Another similarity is that, in contrast with the majority of such proverbs in the sentence literature, proverbs concerning kings and rulers (28.2, 15, 16; 29.4, 12, 14, 26) are not simply submissive and admiring, but are all to some extent critical, and show an awareness of the existence of bad and cruel rulers. There are also, as in ch. 28, references to the education of children (vv. 3, 15, 17).

This chapter, also like ch. 28, lacks a comprehensive structure. However, vv. 12-14 form the nucleus of a loosely formed thematic group. Verses 12 and 14 are clearly related: v. 14 sets out the condition for the continuance of a king's rule—that as judge he treats the poor (*dallîm*) justly; v. 12 points out that in order to do this he must learn to distinguish between true and false evidence or reports. Verse

13, coming between these two verses, has clearly been placed in this position to make the point, or to serve as a reminder, that the poor (here *rāš*) are equal, in the sight of God who has created them, to the influential people who oppress them. (This verse is a close variant of 22.2; and it is probably significant that the variant here has 'oppressor' as against 'rich man' in 22.2, a change made to fit the different context. Other variants in these chapters have undergone similar changes.)

This group may also include vv. 10 and 11. Verse 10 is relevant to the reference to the 'oppressor' in v. 13, and may in fact have been the starting-point for the whole group: it refers to the existence of violence in society, which can only be kept in check by a wise and just king. Verse 14 refers to this royal justice; v. 11 could be seen as advice to a king to acquire wisdom and so not to let anger determine his judgments.

Verses 15-17 are also closely related thematically, and may also be related to the preceding verses. Both vv. 15 and 17 are concerned with the education of children: severe discipline and correction will prevent the disgrace of a child's parents (v. 15); and, more positively, will give repose and pleasure to them (v. 17). Verse 16 seems at first to be simply a general remark about wicked and righteous rulers; but it is so obviously relevant to the preceding group (10-14) that it may be said to link these three verses (15-17) to it. The whole of vv. 10-17 should, then, perhaps be regarded as a distinct group. Kings, like other people, only become wise and just if they have received a wise and strict education.

The theme of education is pursued further in vv. 19-21; but this now includes not only rulers but also those who are at the other end of the social scale: the slaves (*'ebed*, vv. 19, 21). Verse 20 may have been attached to v. 19 because both verses refer to the use of words (*dᵉbārîm*): it is implied in v. 19 that slaves, like children, must be corrected by means of corporal punishment, because they will not pay heed to spoken rebuke; v. 20 also refers to worthless speech, and v. 22 to words spoken in anger. It is probably significant that this section of the book ends with a group of proverbs concerned with the necessity for education of the young, whether of persons born to high estate, ordinary families, or slaves (vv. 19-21), with two proverbs which give an assurance of Yahweh's trustworthiness (v. 25) and justice (v. 26), and finally with two proverbs about the 'two ways'—

of righteousness and wickedness—as uncompromisingly opposed to one another, with no middle way available.

Summary and Conclusions

It has now been demonstrated that there are few verses in these chapters which are entirely isolated, having no kind of connection or affinity with those which immediately precede or follow them. Even in passages that show no sign of the existence of a group structure, there is often a link of some kind from verse to verse, forming an extended chain. It has also been demonstrated that these chapters contain a large number of pairs and small groups which are fairly closely integrated by a common theme or by verbal repetition or paronomasia, or by a combination of these.

With few exceptions, the verses of which these chapters are composed had been in use, before the editorial process began, as independent, self-contained proverbs reflecting a largely agricultural society uninfluenced by the interests of a scribal class. Their formation into groups, however, gave many of them a new interpretation: they became 'wisdom literature'.

There can be no doubt that the purpose of these groups of proverbs is a didactic one. This fact in itself is hardly surprising: it is the nature of a proverb that it is intended to provide guidance to daily living by referring to facts of life learned from experience. But here there is something more precise: an intention to provide and call for parental teaching to guide the lives of boys or young men, similar to that which characterizes the instructions in chs. 1–9. These groups are, in other words, 'instructions', though of a different kind in that they are not integrated poems but have been composed by assembling short proverbs. (The same phenomenon is observable to some extent in the additions that have been made, especially at the end, to some of the original instructions of chs. 1–9.)

The distinctive vocabulary of the verses which introduce the instructions of chs. 1–9 is found fairly frequently here; for example *'āb*, 'father', *'ēm*, 'mother', *mûsār*, 'discipline' but perhaps also implying corporal punishment, *tôkaḥat*, 'rebuke', *tôrâ*, 'teaching'; there are also several references to the 'rod' (*šēbeṭ*) as an instrument of the corporal punishment of young pupils (13.24; 23.13, 14; cf. also 10.13; 26.3; 29.15), a term which does not occur in chs. 1–9.

Altogether these words occur here more than seventy times in some forty verses, together with other similar expressions. These chapters also contain a number of admonitions, to a son (19.20, 27; 27.11) to heed instruction and acquire wisdom, or (again without parallel in chs. 1–9) to a father (19.18; 22.6; 29.17) urging him to discipline his children. In many other passages the same pedagogical intention is clear, though it is expressed in other ways.

There is also evidence that these smaller groups were in many cases combined to form larger ones; the phenomenon of the pivotal verse is one indication of this. Such combinations of groups were made no more haphazardly than in the case of the combination of individual verses to form the smaller groups. There was, then, a gradual process of development into larger and larger groups. Some whole chapters (12, 13, 15, 16, 19, and perhaps 10, 21 and 28) can probably be seen as constituting instructions in the looser sense.

It is, however, important to realize that there is no strict conformity in the ways in which these instructions have been put together. There was clearly considerable variety of editorial practice. One of the clearest signs of this is the widely differing employment of Yahweh proverbs: entirely absent from chs. 13, 26 and 27, frequent in others (chs. 15, 16, 19, 22), rare in chs. 25–29 taken as a whole. Another indication of different methods of composition is the variation in the prominence of specific references to the instruction of children: ch. 19, for example, has many more such references than most other chapters. The difference in the grouping of formal types (such as antithetical and synonymous parallelism) is a further indication of different editorship.

Although the function of the Yahweh proverbs in general was to reinterpret surrounding proverbs with a reminder that human life is controlled and judged by Yahweh, it should not be assumed that the proverbs that do not refer to him are to be regarded as 'secular' or 'godless'. The Yahweh proverbs bring out what was already implicit in the others; they were not—at any rate for the most part—composed especially for that purpose, but they do express a somewhat different tradition with a distinctive emphasis. In some instances (e.g. 15.33) there is a specific concern to emphasize that the instruction given in the accompanying verses conforms to the religious norms of Yahwistic religion. But the impression given by chs. 1–9 that there has been no *systematic* 'Yahweh-edition' of the book is strongly confirmed here.

It is not possible to trace the stages of the composition of these chapters in detail. The generally accepted divisions between chs. 10–15 and 16.1–22.16, and between chs. 25–27 and 28–29, identified largely on the grounds of the predominance of particular syntactical structures, probably do reflect a fairly late stage of composition; chs. 10–15 and 16–22 were subsequently joined by the pivotal 15.33. Prov. 16.1-15 was deliberately made the centre of 10.1–22.16.

The question why the two major collections 10.1–22.16 and 25–29, which resemble one another in many ways, were preserved separately is part of the problem of the final redaction of the book as a whole, and will be considered later. The heading in 25.1 clearly presupposes the existence of the first Solomonic collection (10.1–22.16). The dates of the final redaction of the two collections can obviously not be precisely determined; but there is no reason to doubt the authenticity of the attribution of 25.1 to the 'men (i.e. scribes) of Hezekiah' or to doubt that that heading covers the whole of chs. 25–29 in more or less their present form (some allowance must be made for subsequent additions or rearrangements). Whatever may have been the case with the earlier stages of composition, 25.1 states clearly that these chapters are now 'wisdom literature' in a fully scribal sense.

Chapter 3

PROVERBS 22.17–24.34

Proverbs 22.17–24.22

The question of the composition of these chapters has for many years been discussed mainly in relation to their supposed dependence on an Egyptian source. After the publication of the Egyptian *Instruction of Amenemope*[1] and of Erman's thesis that the Egyptian work was used as a source by the author of Prov. 22.17ff.[2] it was for a long time accepted by almost all scholars that there is a direct literary connection between the two. It is not necessary here to give an account of the discussions which took place;[3] it is sufficient to record that, while a few scholars argued that the Egyptian work is dependent on the Hebrew one or that both were dependent on a common source, the majority favoured the view that it was *Amenemope* which was the model for the biblical text.

Recently, however, serious doubts have been expressed about the theory of a close connection between the two texts by a number of Egyptologists and biblical scholars.[4] J. Ruffle opined that the

1. English translation in F.L. Griffith, 'The Teaching of Amenophis, the Son of Kanekht', *JEA* 12 (1926), pp. 191-231; partial translations in *ANET*, pp. 421-25 and *DOTT*, pp. 172-86. *Amenemope* is now thought to have been written c.1100 BC.

2. A. Erman, 'Eine ägyptische Quelle der "Sprüche Salomos"', *SPAW* 15 (1924), pp. 86-93.

3. See G.E. Bryce, *A Legacy of Wisdom: The Egyptian Contribution to the Wisdom of Israel* (Lewisburg: Bucknell University Press; London: Associated University Presses, 1979), pp. 15-56.

4. D. Römheld (*Wege der Weisheit: Die Lehren Amenemopes und Proverbien 22.17–24.22* [BZAW, 184; Berlin: de Gruyter, 1989]), however, is unconvinced by these. He maintains that Prov. 22.17ff. follows *Amenemope* in its structure and in much of its contents, though it differs in important ways, is creative in some of its ideas and also made use of other Egyptian sources.

similarities can be explained by the fact of the two works having been composed by members of 'related peoples with cognate languages living in similar circumstances and meeting comparable situations'.[5] Bruce[6] was willing to admit no more than that 'The author of the collections of sayings in Prov. 27.17ff has adapted an Egyptian *tradition*' (my italics) 'around which to develop his book'. K.A. Kitchen[7] asserted 'That Prov. xxii 17ff. was copied directly and wholesale is... no longer a tenable assumption'; Krispenz[8] agreed with Ruffle that the similarities can be explained as literary responses to comparable situations within a common culture, pointing out that it is almost impossible in comparing ancient texts to prove direct literary dependence.

Apart from the alleged dependence of parts of the contents of Prov. 22.17ff. on parts of *Amenemope*, much emphasis has been laid on a supposed statement in 22.20 that these chapters consist of thirty sections or admonitions, corresponding to the thirty 'chapters' of the Egyptian work. However, MT in fact makes no reference to the number thirty. The first line of 22.20 reads, 'Have I not written for you *šilšôm*?' (so *kethib*; *qere* has *šālîšîm*). It has been supposed that the consonantal text should be pointed *šᵉlōšîm*, 'thirty'. (It should be noted that even if this conjecture were correct, this would be a strange way of referring to thirty proverbs: for this a noun would be required; the normal phrase would be *šᵉlōšîm dᵉbārîm*, literally 'thirty words'; cf. *dibᵉrê ḥᵃkāmîm*, 'words of the wise', in v. 17.)

In fact the reading of *kethib* (*šilšôm*) is perfectly intelligible (*qere*'s *šālîšîm*, a term denoting a military rank or function, is clearly inappropriate). *šilšôm*, literally '(on) the third day' meaning 'the day before yesterday', elsewhere occurs only together with *tᵉmōl* 'yesterday', in the idiomatic phrase *tᵉmōl šilšōm* and equivalents, literally 'yesterday (and) the day before', but having the sense of 'in the past, formerly'. Its occurrence by itself is thus unique as far as

5. J. Ruffle, 'The Teaching of Amenemope and its Connection with the Book of Proverbs', *TynBul* 28 (1977), p. 37.

6. *Legacy of Wisdom*, p. 85.

7. K.A. Kitchen, 'Egypt and Israel during the First Millennium B.C.', in J.A. Emerton (ed.), *Congress Volume, Jerusalem 1986* (VTSup, 40; Leiden: Brill, 1988), p. 119 n. 70.

8. *Spruchkompositionen im Buch Proverbia* (Europäische Hochschulschriften, 349; Frankfurt: Peter Lang, 1989), pp. 129-31.

extant texts go; but it is reasonable to suppose that it may here have a meaning similar to that of the full phrase. That it does so receives support from the fact that the previous verse (19) also contains a temporal expression, *hayyôm*, 'today' or 'now'.

The line may therefore be rendered 'Did I not write to you earlier...?', meaning 'I have (certainly) written earlier...' This may be taken to refer to some previous instruction composed (or perhaps transcribed) by the same writer to the same pupil.[9]

A further point is that those who have attempted to show that 22.17–24.22 does in fact comprise thirty distinct sections have been too hasty in their assessments. In fact there is strong evidence that this is not the case; indeed, as has been shown by Niccacci,[10] these chapters did not originally constitute a literary unit at all. He showed that 22.17–23.11 forms a single unit containing ten units or admonitions, but that 23.12 and 26 are new introductions (though they are generally counted among the 'thirty' sections) marking the beginnings of quite separate instructions. In fact, as will be argued below, there are even more distinct instructions here than even Niccacci supposed: 23.19, 23.22-26, 24.3-4 and 24.13-14 also mark new beginnings. But there are not thirty.

Even as regards contents it can be shown that these chapters are not modelled on *Amenemope*. It is generally admitted that the thematic parallels end at 23.11 (with perhaps one or two exceptions), long before the supposed thirtieth admonition is reached; and it is also difficult to explain why even in the first part up to 23.11 the order in which the themes occur is completely different from that found in *Amenemope*. That there is much material in these chapters which has affinities with various Egyptian instructions cannot be denied; but the notion of a close dependence on *Amenemope* must be given up.

As has already been adumbrated, 22.17–24.22 contains instructions similar to those of chs. 1–9. It consists mainly of admonitions, generally with motive clauses, together with a few passages in different

---

9. The reading *šᵉlōšîm*, 'thirty', is rejected also by some other scholars, e.g. W. Richter, *Recht und Ethos: Versuch einer Ortung des weisheitlichen Mahnspruches* (SANT, 15; Munich: Kösel, 1966), p. 37; McKane, *Proverbs*, p. 372. Ruffle ('The Teaching of Amenemope', pp. 54-55) considers that it 'should be treated with some reserve'.

10. A. Niccacci, 'Proverbi 22.17–23.11', *Studii Biblici Franciscani Liber Annuus* (Jerusalem) 29 (1979), pp. 42-72.

styles but with the same educational purpose. It begins with an extended
introduction (22.17-21) comparable with 1.1-6. There is an address to
'my son' in 23.15, 19, 26, 24.13, 21; and although this expression
does not occur in 22.17–23.11, both the style and the contents of those
verses make it clear that they also are addressed by a teacher to a
pupil. Prov. 23.22 and 25 mention father and mother together (cf.
1.8; 6.20). Prov. 23.13-14 is addressed to a father, urging him to
exercise strict discipline over his children, a theme also found in the
less formal instructions of the 'sentence literature' (13.24; 19.18).

The close affinity between these instructions and those of chs. 1–9 is
shown by the frequent use of identical (or in some cases equivalent)
words and phrases in the introductory sections.

1. 'Incline your ear (*haṭ 'oznekā*), 22.17, occurs also in 4.20;
    5.1.
2. The command to 'hear' (*šᵉmaʿ*) the father's words (22.17) is
    found (occasionally in the plural) in 1.8; 4.1, 10; 5.7; 7.24.
3. 'If you keep them in your belly' (*kî-tišmᵉrēm bᵉbiṭnekā*) in
    22.18 is reminiscent of similar phrases in 4.21; 6.21; 7.3.
4. 'Keep' (*šāmar*) is also used in the above connection in 4.21,
    5.2, 7.1, and its equivalent *nāṣar* in 3.1, 5.2 and 6.20.
5. The root *nʿm* (*nāʿîm*, 'pleasant', 22.18), used of the effect of
    treasuring the teacher's words, is also used in chs. 1–9: 2.10
    states that 'knowledge will be pleasant' (*yinʿām*), and 3.17
    that Wisdom's ways are 'ways of pleasantness' (*darᵉkê
    nōʿam*). This was evidently a device of the teacher to
    persuade the pupil to accept joyfully the discipline imposed
    on him.
6. In 23.19, 'and direct your heart in the way' (*wᵉ 'aššēr
    badderek libbekā*) is reminiscent of Wisdom's call to 'walk in
    the way of understanding' (*'iššᵉrû bᵉderek bînâ*), 9.6 and 'and
    do not enter the path of the wicked' (*wᵉ 'al-tᵉ 'aššēr bᵉderek
    rāʿîm*) in 4.14. (*'šr*, 'proceed', *piel* 'direct', is a rare verb
    which occurs only four times elsewhere in the Old
    Testament.)
7. The admonition in 23.23 to 'Get (*qᵉnēh*)...wisdom' is
    identical with that in 4.5, 7.
8. The statement in 24.3 that 'By wisdom a house is built'
    (*bᵉhokmâ yibbāneh bāyit*) corresponds to 9.1, 'Wisdom has

built her house' (cf. also 14.1). (It should be noted that as in the instructions in chs. 1–9 in their augmented form, wisdom is regarded in some of these introductory verses as the equivalent of the father's instruction.)

Some of the *themes* of these instructions are the same as those of some of the instructions of chs. 1–9; others coincide with the themes of proverbs in the sentence literature, although they are more extensive and mainly in the form of admonitions.

Warnings against associating with criminals in acts of violence, and against envying them—often a preliminary to active participation with them—is a main theme of chs. 1–9 (1.8-19; 3.31; 4.14-19); this is also true of the chapters under present discussion: 22.24-25; 23.17-18; 24.8-9; 24.15-16. The fact that this theme is treated more than once may be an indication that such crimes were particularly prevalent at the time when the instructions were composed; but it is also confirmation, as in the case of chs. 1–9, that a number of different instructions are involved here. On the other hand, there is only one warning against association with immoral women (23.27-28). This has the word *nokriyyâ*, probably 'adulteress', in common with 2.16, 6.24 and 7.5, but otherwise has affinities with 22.14, where also the woman is described as a 'deep pit' (*šûḥâ ʿamuqqâ*). The remaining themes are either similar to those in the sentence literature or unique to these instructions. It would appear that there was a considerable stock of themes available both to the collectors of individual proverbs and to the authors of instructions.

Proverbs 22.17–23.11

Niccacci has shown that 22.17–23.11 is a single instruction that has been carefully constructed. It consists of ten sections (22.22-23, 24-25, 26-27, 28, 29; 23.1-3, 4-5, 6-8, 9, 10-11) preceded by an introduction (22.17-21). These are not all in the form of admonitions. The first and last parts of the instruction (22.22-28 and 23.4-11), comprising the first and the last four sections, are admonitions, all concerned with actions to be avoided: oppression of the poor, association with the violent, giving pledges, moving boundaries, slaving to get wealth, dining with misers, talking to the stupid, moving boundaries (again!). All have motive clauses except 22.28. Niccacci argues that there is an inclusio in that, although the repeated admonition (about moving boundaries) is found in numbers 4 and 10 and not 1 and 10, the first and the last have a virtually identical motive clause.[11] He sees the final admonition (23.10-11) as rounding out the whole, picking up in this way both numbers 1 and 4. It is interesting that no less than three of these sections show concern for the poor, a theme which does not occur at all in chs. 1–9. There are stylistic affinities between several of the admonitions. Prov. 22.22-23, 23.6-7, 23.10-11 all have *'al-...kî...*('Do not...for...') and 22.24-25 *'al...pen...*('Do not...lest...').

Niccacci[12] observes that the themes of the two central sections, numbers 5 and 6 (22.29 and 23.1-3) are of a different kind from those of the others: they are directly concerned to give advice to a young man which will help him to achieve his social and material ambitions. But his argument that they provide a precise clue to the background and purpose of the instruction as *professional* advice to an ambitious would-be courtier or civil servant, as are many of the Egyptian instructions, rests on slender grounds.

Prov. 22.29ab, a lesson taught by means of an example ('Do you see. . . ?'), proposes as a model of conduct 'a man who is skillful in his work' (*'îš māhîr bim^{e}lā'ktô*). Niccacci sees the word *māhîr* as referring to an official, a member of the scribal class; but this is not necessarily the case. The adjective *māhîr*, 'swift, alert', occurs in only three other verses in the Old Testament. In two of these (Ezra 7.6; Ps. 45.1 [2]) it qualifies the word 'scribe' in the phrase *sôpēr/sōpēr māhîr*, ' a skillful scribe'; this may have been a stock phrase in W. Semitic: it appears in Aramaic (*spr ḥkym wmhyr* in *The Words of Ahiqar* 1.1).[13] But *māhîr* is an adjective; and, in Hebrew at least, it is not known to have been used as a noun with the meaning 'scribe'. On the contrary, in the only other occurrence in the Old Testament, Isa. 16.5, it is used of the messianic king, who is said to be *m^{e}hîr ṣedeq*, 'swift (or eager) to do right' (the basic meaning of *mhr* is 'to hasten').

Nor does the word *m^{e}lā'kâ*, 'work', ever specifically refer to the

---

11. Prov. 22.23a has *kî-yhwh yārîb rîbām*, 'for Yahweh will plead their cause'; 23.11b has *hû'-yārîb 'et-rîbām 'ittāk*, 'he will plead their cause against you'. Prov. 22.28a and 23.10a (*'al-tasēg g^{e}bûl 'ôlām*) are identical.

12. 'Proverbi 22.17–23.11', pp. 63-65.

13. A.E. Cowley, *Aramaic Papyri of the Fifth Century B.C.* (Oxford: Clarendon Press, 1923), p. 212; translation on p. 220.

work of a scribe. It is a general term for work of any kind, though frequently used of skilled work; it is used, for example, of the skilled work of the men who made the furnishings for the tabernacle (Exod. 31). Further, the words 'he will stand before kings' does not necessarily refer to the position of a scribe or courtier: there is no reference to a specific king, and the expression is a hyperbolic promise that a person who skilfully or eagerly does whatever work falls to him will make a success of his life.[14] (The third line of this verse adds little to the sense of the previous lines and itself makes little sense: no-one would be ambitious to 'stand before', that is, serve, obscure men. The line may be a gloss; but if so it is probably corrupt.)

Nor does 23.1-3 necessarily refer to a courtier. These verses, on how to behave when invited to dinner by a 'ruler' (*môšēl*), show clearly that the instruction is addressed to a young man of the upper class like the instructions of chs. 1–9, a young man who, however, is still somewhat gauche and needs advice on social behaviour; this is a standard topic of wisdom literature, occurring in the Egyptian instructions of *Kagemni*, *Ptahhotep* and *Amenemope*, and reaching down to the Hellenistic period: it occurs also in Ecclus. 31.12-18. These verses may well have been written with an eye to smoothing the path of the ambitious pupil bent on getting to the top, and could only be of use in a class of society which gives dinner-parties; but there is no more specific indication of the circumstances. It was evidently a matter of importance to the guest that he should make a good impression on his influential host. It may be remarked that these two passages (22.29 and 23.1-3) are not as unlike the others as Niccacci supposes: others (at least 22.24-25 and 26-27) are no less designed to further the pupil's future career.

Although in their present form the ten sections of 22.17–23.11, now gathered under a single heading, constitute a single instruction, it is possible that they originally existed independently. Unlike the (original) instructions of chs. 1–9 they differ considerably in form and length. The first three and the last (22.22-23, 24-25, 26-27; 23.10-11) are single, four-line admonitions including a motive clause;

---

14. See my comments on proverbs in chs. 10–29 which refer to kings in *Wealth and Poverty in the Book of Proverbs* (JSOTSup, 99; Sheffield: JSOT Press, 1990), pp. 45-59.

23.9 is also a single admonition with motive clause, but has only two lines; 22.28 is a single admonition with no motive clause. Three admonitions are somewhat longer, with more elaborate details: 23.1-3, 4-5, 6-8. Of these, 23.1-3 begins with a temporal clause setting the scene. One passage (22.29) is not formally an admonition but uses the device of a question to put a hypothetical case. The repetition of the same theme (the moving of boundaries) in 22.28 and 23.10-11 (compare the repeated instructions on the adulteress in chs. 1–9) is also difficult to account for if the whole of these verses was composed as a single instruction.

In 22.17–23.11 there are just two references to Yahweh (22.19, 23) and one to a 'redeemer' (*gō'ēl*, 23.11) which appears to be an indirect allusion to him. In all other respects the instruction has the character of a father's instruction to his son as in the original instructions in chs. 1–9: the speaker refers to 'my words' and 'my teaching' (22.17) and commends them to the pupil as 'pleasant' (v. 18). The question arises whether, as in the case of chs. 1–9, these references to God are subsequent additions.

In 22.19 the first line, which speaks of trust in Yahweh, is somewhat loosely attached (with an infinitive clause) to what precedes, and may also be said to interrupt the discourse, since vv. 19b-21 resume the first person address of the teacher. It is possible that the reference to Yahweh in 22.23 is also an addition to the admonition: it occurs in a motive clause; and an admonition with no motive clause would not be unique in this instruction (cf. v. 28).[15] The same applies to 23.11,

15. See the discussion of motive clauses in B. Gemser, 'The Importance of the Motive Clause in Old Testament Law', in G.W. Anderson *et al.* (eds.), *Congress Volume, Copenhagen 1953* (VTSup, 1; Leiden: Brill, 1953), pp. 50-66. Although in the case of the laws Gemser believed that the use of motive clauses was probably very ancient (though peculiar to Israel), he noted that in the later laws of Deuteronomy there is a much higher proportion of them than in the Covenant Code (Exod. 21–23), a fact that presumably points to a growing tendency to attach them to earlier laws that originally had none. In fact, here in Prov. 22.22-23 the admonition itself (v. 22) is couched in a form similar to that of legal formularies, and is closely related to a law in the Covenant Code (Exod. 23.6) to which no motive clause is attached, although clearly Yahweh's sanction is to be understood. The lack of such a clause attached to the original admonition of Prov. 22.22 would not, of course, mean that Yahweh was not thought to be relevant: v. 23 would have been added as a *reminder* of his involvement. The whole admonition (vv. 22-23) as it now stands is expressed virtually in legal terms (except for *'al-*, 'Do not...' rather than *lō'*, 'Thou

which is the motive clause attached to v. 10. (It may also be noted that the different ways of referring to God in 22.23 and 23.11 may be a further indication of different authorship.)

It should further be noted that in 22.17–23.11 there is no trace of an identification of the teacher's words with a personified Wisdom such as is to be found in some of the augmented instructions of chs. 1–9: the word 'wisdom' does not occur at all.

Prov. 22.17-21 is a preface or introduction, probably originally to 22.22–23.11; but these verses are now to be seen as introducing the whole of 22.22–24.22—that is, as far as the next heading at 24.33. Verse 17 in MT reads, 'Incline your ear and hear words of wise men (*dib^erê ḥ^akāmîm*), and apply your mind to my knowledge'; but the widely held view that 'words of wise men' was originally not part of v. 17 but constituted the heading which preceded it is certainly correct. This section of the book has no other heading, and the heading to the next section, 'These also are words of wise men' (24.23), confirms the hypothesis. The heading in 22.17 was also certainly added at a fairly late stage in the editorial process; but if, as has been argued above, these chapters are the work of a number of different authors, the plural 'wise men' is appropriate. But it cannot be part of the words of the teachers themselves, who would not refer to themselves in this way.

This preface has been compared with 1.1-6 and also with the beginning of *Amenemope*; but the closest affinities are with the introductions to the instructions of chs. 1–9 (see the remarks on their terminology, p. 13 above).

Verse 20, 'Have I not written for you...?', is the only reference to writing in the whole of the book of Proverbs. As has been argued above, it refers to an instruction in written form given to the pupil at an earlier date, now not extant. Now (*hayyôm*, 'today', v. 19) the teacher presents the pupil with a further instruction (*hôda'tîkā*, literally 'I have made known to you', is to be understood as having a present meaning; see GKC 106 i for this use of the perfect tense).

In v. 21, 'to bring back a reliable report to anyone who may send you' (*l^ehāšîb '^amārîm '^emet l^ešōl^ḥêkā*) literally 'to return words [which are] true' [see GKC 131 c] to those who send you') has been

___

shalt not...'): note the legal phrase '(he) will plead their cause' (*yārîb rîbām*) in v. 23.

supposed, especially in view of a passage in the Egyptian instruction of *Ptahhotep* ('Be thoroughly reliable when he sends you' [*ANET*, p. 413]) and of *Amenemope* 1.5, 'to direct a report to one who has sent him' (*ANET*, p. 421) to allude to a specific function of the apprentice official or scribe (so, e.g., McKane, Plöger); but such a precise connotation is by no means necessary. There are several references to the sending to and fro of messengers who report back the replies to their messages in the 'sentence literature' of Proverbs (10.26; 13.17; 26.6); and in those cases there is certainly no question of scribal or official messengers. The carrying of messages necessary for the conduct of business or for family or personal reasons was a necessary and frequent practice in the ancient world, and all these three passages in Proverbs, like 22.21, stress the importance of employing a reliable and intelligent messenger. At whatever level of society the carrying out of messages by a young man or boy would be a good test of his competence.

Proverbs 23.12–24.22

In contrast with 22.17–23.11, these verses have not been organized into a single literary unit. They contain a number of short instructions, some provided with introductions; but they also contain material of other kinds, though all of an educational nature. They are probably unconnected appendixes that have been added piecemeal to the more integrated material that precedes them.

There appear to be five passages which may be identified as *introductions* to following admonitions: they vary considerably in length and are not all in the 'classical' or 'standard' form. They are 23.12-16, 23.19, 23.22-26, 24.3-4 and 24.13-14. They serve to mark out the divisions of the material; the verses that follow them contain the main bodies of concrete admonitions.

Prov. 23.12-16 is unusual in that an address to a father (vv. 13-14) appears to have been embedded in the usual address by a father to his son (vv. 12, 15-16). Plöger in his commentary has attempted to solve this problem by arguing that v. 12 is not the beginning of a new section but the conclusion of the foregoing instruction; vv. 13-14 also belong to what precedes, constituting an appendix standing outside the body of that instruction. He considers that the new section begins only with v. 15. However, there are in fact no other examples of such a *conclusion* to an instruction. Moreover, this kind of change of standpoint is not unique in this kind of material. Advice addressed to a parent occurs occasionally in the sentence literature of Proverbs (19.18; 22.6; 29.17); and as for the abrupt alternation between address to son and address to father, there is an example of precisely the same phenomenon in the *Words of Ahiqar* ll. 8-82 in a passage whose wording is so similar to these verses that a direct connection between the two has often been suggested.[16]

The father's appeal to the pupil in v. 12 is in standard form (cf. the introductory verses to instructions in chs. 1–9). Verse 15 addresses the pupil as 'My son', a term regularly employed in chs. 1–9 but, interestingly, entirely missing from 22.17–23.11. The statements in vv. 15-16, that if the pupil acquires wisdom the father will rejoice, occur several times in the sentence literature. The body of the instruction, consisting of a single admonition, is comprised in vv. 17-18.

Prov. 23.19 is another introduction also addressing the pupil as 'my son' and using the standard phraseology familiar from chs. 1–9. It also contains a single admonition (vv. 20-21). Prov. 23.22-26 is almost certainly composite. Verses 22 and 26 are in fairly standard form, but vv. 23-25 are probably secondary. Verse 24, expressed in the third person, appears to be an originally isolated proverb to which a more personal note has been added in v. 25. Verse 23 is an obvious addition to v. 22 associating wisdom with the parental teaching, using words also found in 4.5, 7. This introduction was thus quite short in its original form. The body of the instruction consists of vv. 27-28, but it is in the form of statements rather than of an admonition.

Prov. 24.3-4 appears to be introductory to vv. 5-9, but is not presented in the usual form. It is an elaboration of the statement found elsewhere (9.1; 14.1) about the house built by Wisdom. The purpose of v. 4, however, is to persuade the pupil (or reader—there is no direct address) of the material rewards and pleasure (*nā'îm*) to be obtained by the possession of wisdom, and so may be considered as equivalent to the parental introduction. But the verses which follow, constituting the body of the teaching, are in the form of proverbs

16. Cowley, *Aramaic Papyri*, pp. 214-15; translation on p. 222: 'The son who is trained and taught, and on whose feet the fetter is put [shall prosper]. Do not withhold your son from the rod, if you cannot keep him from wickedness. If I beat you, my son, you will not die, and if I leave you to your heart [you will not live]'. (The words in square brackets are conjectural; the papyrus is damaged.)

rather than of admonitions. Verse 6 adopts the phrase 'But it is by wise guidance that you make war' from 20.18.

Prov. 24.13-14 is addressed to 'my son', but is not expressed in the standard formula. The advice to 'eat honey', like the other references in the book to honey (16.24; 25.16; 25.27), is not intended to be taken literally: the sweetness is used as an analogy for the 'sweetness' of wisdom. These verses, which are concerned entirely with wisdom without any mention of the father's teaching, are, however, clearly intended as an introduction to the instruction that follows, which is the most extensive in these chapters, comprising three (and probably four)[17] distinct admonitions, and extending to the end of this section of the book.

There is one further short instruction (a single admonition) in these chapters: 24.1-2; but it entirely lacks an introduction. It is quite isolated: there is no way in which it can be connected either with what precedes or with what follows.

Among these admonitions are interspersed two passages which do not follow the lines of the 'classical' instruction, although they contain elements of the admonition: 23.29-35 and 24.10-12.

Prov. 23.29-35 has no parental introduction. It begins (vv. 29-30) with a riddle.[18] Six questions enquire about the identity of a certain class of person who suffers in a variety of ways; v. 30 gives the answer: it is the drunkard. These two verses, which make a complete point of their own, may have been attached subsequently to vv. 31-35, although they could be considered as constituting a lively introduction to them. Verse 31 is an admonition; v. 32 its motive clause. But vv. 33-35 appear to be a continuation of this, elaborating its point in a vivid and humorous way. These verses are somewhat reminiscent of the vivid scene in 7.6-23.

Prov. 24.10-12 also has no introductory section. It has been interpreted in a number of ways. But v. 11 begins with an imperative, *haṣṣēl*, 'Rescue!', and the second line of that verse has a similar

---

17. On vv. 21-22 see below.

18. Von Rad, *Weisheit in Israel*, pp. 32-33 (ET p. 18) and McKane, *Proverbs*, p. 393 see these verses as having the character of a riddle ('a challenge to discover the answer which will accommodate all the clues', McKane). But von Rad (p. 56 [ET p. 37]) also characterizes them as a numerical proverb employed for educational purposes as a 'school question'. There are other examples in Ecclus 10.19; 22.14.

connotation.[19] Verse 12 is the equivalent of a motive clause, brushing aside protestations of ignorance and affirming that God, who observes human character, will not fail to punish those who fail to do what is commanded in v. 11. Verse 10 has been thought to be an isolated verse, but is probably related to the following verses, warning against cowardice or faintheartedness.[20]

That these verses (23.12–24.22) are of diverse origins is confirmed—as in the case of the instructions in chs. 1–9—by the fact that at least two of the themes are repeated: the warning against envying the wicked occurs three times (23.17-18; 24.1-2; 24.19-20) and that against drunkenness twice (23.20-21; 23.29-35). There are also similarities between the admonition against those who plan to do evil (24.8-9) and against violence (24.15-16). (The other themes are the superiority of wisdom to physical strength [24.5-6], rescuing the victims of violence [24.10-12],[21] rejoicing in the fall of personal enemies [24.17-18] and the duty to fear Yahweh and the king [24.21-22].)

The only instruction of substantial length occurs at the end of the section: 24.13-22.[22] It may have been placed here to give a semblance of order to the whole section which begins in 23.12. The admonition in vv. 21-22 to fear the destructive power of both Yahweh and the king may be intended to sum up the instructions in a way reminiscent of the combination of the two topics in 16.1-15. The reference to the king may perhaps have played a part in the placing of chs. 25–29, which begin (25.2-7) with a section on kings.

---

19. *'im-taḥśôk* here expresses a wish rather than a command: 'May you spare... !'; so GKC151e; S.R. Driver, *A Treatise on the Use of the Tenses in Hebrew* (Oxford: Clarendon Press, 1892), p. 142; R.J. Williams, *Hebrew Syntax: An Outline* (Toronto: Toronto University Press, 1967), p. 458.

20. See the commentaries for discussions of these difficult verses.

21. *lᵉqūḥîm lammāwet* in v. 11 means not 'being taken away to death' but 'seized for death', that is, 'subject to a murderous attack'. It cannot refer to persons being led away for official execution, whether guilty or not: if they were innocent it would be impossible for the young man to rescue them from the authorities, and if they were guilty it would obviously not be in accordance with God's will to attempt to do so. These people are victims of violent assault by street gangs, of the kind of violence against which the pupil is warned in some of the other instructions.

22. The recurrence of 'My son' in v. 21 is a resumption of the original address in v. 13 rather than the beginning of a new instruction (compare its use in 1.10 and 1.15). Verses 21-22 may, however, be an appendix to vv. 13-20 bringing the entire section to a conclusion.

The instructions in 23.12–24.22 are sparing in their references to God: there are only four of these, and only three mention Yahweh by name. There are no references at all to God in 23.19–24.9, which comprise five of the instructions. Two references occur in the same instruction (24.13-22); of these, v. 18 is in a motive clause; that in v. 21 may not be original to the instruction but, as has already been suggested, may be part of a general conclusion to this section of the book. The reference in 23.17 is probably original as it occurs in the motive clause to a brief admonition which consists altogether only of two lines and so could hardly be omitted. The reference in 24.12 to God simply as 'he who weighs hearts' (cf. 16.2; 21.2) and as 'he who keeps watch over you' (*nōṣēr napšᵉkā*) also constitutes the equivalent of a motive clause and is probably original.

There are four references to wisdom: 23.23; 24.3, 7; 24.14. In these, wisdom is presented as a desirable acquisition but not fully personified. Prov. 23.23, as noted above, is an addition to v. 22 associating wisdom with the parental teaching. Prov. 24.3-7, however, is solely concerned with wisdom, and the references in vv. 3 and 7 may be intended to form a framework to the intervening verses. Prov. 24.14 is part of the introduction to the instruction which follows and is to be seen as the father's advice to his son. These references to wisdom, although they occur only in three of the instructions in these chapters, mark a contrast with 22.17–23.11 in which there are none at all.

Proverbs 24.23-34

These twelve verses, as is clearly shown by the heading 'These also are from wise men' (*gam-'ēlleh laḥᵃkāmîm*), are simply a further appendix to the 'words of wise men' which marks the beginning of 22.17ff. This is, or should be, obvious; but the widespread belief that 22.17ff. is modelled on *Amenemope* has somewhat obscured the point.[23]

23. From 22.17–24.22 onwards LXX orders the sections of the book otherwise than MT: in LXX, 22.17–24.22 is followed by 30.1–14 and then in turn by versions of MT's 24.23-24; 30.15-33; 31.1-9; chs. 25–29; 31.10-31. The heading to 24.23-34 in LXX also differs from that in MT. It would appear that MT's *laḥᵃkāmîm*, which could mean '*for* wise men' but must certainly be intended (in view of *gam-*, 'also' and general probability) to mean 'of', that is, '*by* wise men', has been interpreted by

This section contains quite miscellaneous materials; only vv. 27-29 are admonitions. There is no introduction with an address by father to pupil; there are also no references either to Yahweh or to wisdom. There is no discernible structure, although only two topics are treated: the importance of honesty and impartiality in the administration of justice (vv. 23b-26, 28 and probably also 29[24]) and advice to members of a farming community about the proper administration of their farms (vv. 27, 30-34). The two topics are intermingled. In contrast with 22.17–24.22, these elements point to the same social and economic background as that of the sentence literature,[25] although the material has evidently been assembled for a literate readership.

Verse 23b, like v. 29, is a statement in prose, and expresses a legal principle. Verses 24-25 elaborate this, setting out the consequences of obedience and disobedience to it. Verse 26 is short and perhaps defective; but 'returning honest words' (*mēšîb dᵉbārîm nᵉkōḥîm*) may refer, like v. 28, to the speech of an honest witness. 'Kisses the lips' is unique imagery, but may mean that the honest witness is as welcome to an innocent accused person as the kisses of a lover.

Verses 27 and 30-34 are probably to be taken literally. Agricultural work is not to be undertaken without due preparation; 'building a house' may refer either to the construction of a farmhouse or to the founding of a family. The subject of vv. 30-34 is the familiar one of the necessity of diligent application to one's work; compare 6.6-11. It is an example of how a single topic can be expanded and presented in a vivid way as a teaching device. The moral is the same as in 10.4, 13.4, 15.19, 20.4, 13 and several other proverbs in the sentence literature. The form is that of a short moral tale comparable with 4.3ff., 7.6-23 and Ps. 37.35-36, in which a teacher recounts his own experiences—whether real or fictional—in order to make a point. Verses 33-34, containing the moral, are virtually identical with

LXX in the former sense: 'And these things I say to you (that are) wise, to learn (them)' (*tauta de legō humin tois sophois epigignōskein*). On the question of the differences between the order of LXX and that of MT in general, see the final chapter of this book.

24. Verse 29, a warning against taking revenge, is similar to 20.22a. It has no poetical form and appears to be prose. Although it could have a general application it may be a comment on v. 28: the seeking of revenge for supposed past injuries would be an obvious motive for giving false witness against a neighbour.

25. See my *Wealth and Poverty in the Book of Proverbs*, pp. 75-77.

6.10-11, an indication that we are dealing here with material generally current in society.

To sum up: this section of the book (22.17–24.34) consists of a well-organized instruction (22.17–23.11) comparable with chs. 1–9, followed by two appendixes (23.12–24.22 and 24.23-34). These appendixes have been placed here because they also contain instructional material, though they both lack organization and structure and are mixed in content. Prov. 23.12–24.22 contains a number of distinct introductions which suggest separate composition, but has no single heading indicative of its having had a separate existence as a whole before being placed in its present position. Prov. 24.23-34 originated in part in quite separate circles from the earlier instructional material in the book. It has a single comprehensive heading, and may once have existed as a separate short collection despite its very miscellaneous character.

Chapter 4

PROVERBS 30–31

The material in these two final chapters of Proverbs is also of a miscellaneous nature. There are only two headings in the text, at 30.1 and 31.1; but it is clear that these were not intended to cover the whole of the subsequent material. In MT (though not in LXX) the headings attribute the material immediately following to non-Israelites.

As has already been noted, the order in which the material subsequent to 24.22 is arranged in LXX is quite different from its order in MT: it corresponds to MT's 30.1-14, 24.23-34, 30.15-33, 31.1-9, chs. 25–29 and 31.10-31. The possible implications of this divergence for the composition of the book as a whole will be considered in the final chapter of this book. But the fact that LXX separates 30.1-14 from 30.15-33 is of importance for the study of the composition of ch. 30.

It is of course not possible to know in what order these groups of verses occurred in LXX's *Vorlage*; but as no reason is apparent why LXX should have changed that order, it has been concluded by some scholars that the LXX text—here and in other chapters—reflects a time when the order of the material was not yet fixed. That 30.1-14 and 15-33 were originally unconnected is generally accepted by modern scholars, on the grounds of their contents.

Proverbs 30.1-14: The 'Words of Agur'

These verses present some of the most difficult problems in the whole book. The fact that LXX appears to have regarded them as a unit does not mean that they are in fact necessarily a single composition. In fact, there is strong evidence, with regard both to style and content, that we have here a core 'oracle' to which several additions have been made. In vv. 1b-3 a speaker refers to himself in the first person singular.

Verses 4-6, however, are in a quite different style. They are at least partly derivative. The questions in v. 4 belong to a situation of controversy; they strongly resemble, and in some detail, God's devastating and unanswerable question to Job in Job 38, and are also reminiscent of Isa. 40.12. Verse 5 may be derived from a verse in the Song of David in 2 Samuel (2 Sam. 22.31 = Ps. 18.30 [31]); v. 6a recalls Deut. 4.2 and 12.32. The prayer in vv. 7-9, in which a speaker (again in the first person) makes two requests of God, has been classed as a numerical saying similar to those of which the second half of the chapter (vv. 15-13) is largely composed; 30.11-14 is certainly such a numerical proverb. It should also be noted that in vv. 1-9 God is referred to in three (or four) different ways: as *'ēl* (v. 1b, possibly: see below); as *qᵉdōšîm*, 'the Holy One' (v. 3); as *'ᵉlôah*, 'God' (v. 5); and as Yahweh (v. 9).

Some scholars have argued that at least vv. 1-9 are the result of attempts to supplement or correct an original 'oracle' and to give it a kind of unity. Sauer[1] saw the whole chapter in this light. Franklyn[2] sees vv. 1-9 as a unit. Plöger, on the other hand, restricts the *Words of Agur* to vv. 1-4, with vv. 5-6 as an addition to them. McKane considers that they extend no further than v. 3 or possibly v. 4.

There is, then, no agreement about the composition and unity of these verses. Versus 1b-3 may certainly be regarded, in spite of the difficulties of v. 1, as a unit. From v. 6 onwards there are signs of the use of catchwords to join one unit to another. Thus although v. 10 is an isolated proverb, the use of the word 'curse' there may have been the reason for its placing after v. 9 with its reference to profaning the name of God. The reference to falsehood in v. 8 may be intended to echo the mention of lying in v. 6. Verses 5 and 6 have no linking catchwords, but these 'quotations' may have been intended to clinch the reference to the omnipotence of the creator-God in v. 4.

But it is difficult to discover any original continuity or progression of thought in these verses as a whole. Detailed exegesis is not within the scope of the present study; but reference must be made to v. 1b:

---

1. G. Sauer, *Die Sprüche Agurs: Untersuchungen zur Herkunft, Verbreitung und Bedeutung einer biblischer Stilform unter besonderer Berücksichtigung von Proverbia c. 30* (BWANT, 84; Stuttgart: Kohlhammer, 1963), pp. 92-112.

2. P. Franklyn, 'The Sayings of Agur in Proverbs 30: Piety or Scepticism?', *ZAW* 95 (1983), pp. 238-52.

these opening words of the speaker, far from providing a clue to the verses which follow, must be regarded as unintelligible. Many attempts have been made to understand them, either as they stand in the Hebrew text, or by repointing or emending them; but there is no agreement at all among scholars about their meaning.[3] It is therefore almost impossible to grasp the intention of the passage as a whole. Verses 1-9 are probably best regarded as the result of a series of attempts to integrate an originally non-Israelite and non-Yahwistic saying into the sphere of Yahwistic wisdom teaching. Verses 11-14 appear to have no connection with the foregoing passages.

Proverbs 30.15-33

In one sense these verses do not present any special compositional problems. They are basically a collection of examples of a particular kind of proverb generally known as the numerical proverb[4] of which 6.16-19 is also an example.[5] However, whereas 6.16-19 is a Yahweh saying, there is no mention of God in these verses at all.

The collection, to which a few examples of other kinds of material have been added, is clearly not an original unit. No attempt has been made to maintain a unity of style or a logical sequence of content. Several different types of numerical proverb have been mixed together, apparently at random. There is, however, a link—though

---

3. MT has *nᵉ'ūm haggeber lᵉ'îtî'ēl lᵉ'îtî'ēl wᵉ'ūkāl*. As pointed, this might mean 'The man says to Ithiel, to Ithiel and Ukal', and this is how the older English translations (AV, RV, followed by RSV) render it. There is a proper name Ithiel in Neh. 11.7; a name Ukal, however, is less probable. Modern commentaries and versions reject this translation on various grounds. C.C. Torrey, 'Proverbs, Chapter 30', *JBL* 73 (1954), pp. 93-96 believed the verse to be in Aramaic (!): 'Oracle of the man. I am not God, I am not God that I might be capable'; Gemser, *Sprüche Salomos*, 1937[1]: 'Saying of the man who has struggled with God... and prevailed'; Gemser, *Sprüche Salomos*, 1962[2]: 'Saying of the man. I am incapable, O God... and can I understand?'; McKane, *Proverbs*, 'The utterance of the man. There is no God... and I am exhausted'; Franklyn, 'The Sayings of Agur': 'Oracle of the man. I am weary, O God... and I perish'; Plöger, *Sprüche Salomos*: 'Utterance of the man who has struggled with God. I have struggled, O God, so that I might grasp it' (so also Sauer); NRSV: 'Thus says the man: I am weary, O God... How can I prevail?'; NEB, REB: 'This is the great man's very word: I am weary and worn out'.

4. On the numerical proverb, see Sauer, *Die Sprüche Agurs*.

5. See pp. 50-51 above.

not an original one—with the immediately preceding verses in that vv. 11-14, and probably, in a looser sense, vv. 7-9 are also numerical proverbs. Verses 15-33 may therefore be regarded as an appendix or a series of appendixes to vv. 1-14, inserted here because of this feature shared with the last part of that section.[6]

Four of the items (vv. 15b-16, 18-19, 21-23, 29-31) belong to a particular type known as the 'graded numerical proverb',[7] which begins with a reference to two consecutive numbers (here 'Three [things]. . . [and] four', with slight variations—examples elsewhere have different sequential numbers) and names a common characteristic of the items that follow. Verses 11-14 also list four items (unpleasant types of person), but here there is no introductory formula and no specific enumeration; rather, each item begins with the same word *dôr*, elsewhere frequently rendered by 'generation' but here meaning 'a group or kind of persons who...' Verses 24-28 begin with the formula 'Four things' followed by a statement about a common characteristic (small yet wise), but lack the double enumeration ('three...four'). This proverb is also longer than the other examples: each item occupies two poetical lines, the first referring to a point of apparent weakness, the second to the 'wisdom' of the four animals in question. In vv. 18-19, as in vv. 11-14, each item begins with the same word (here *derek*, 'way'), although this proverb also has the 'standard' introductory formula.

Some verses lack the standard form altogether. Verses 7-9 and 15a may have been included here because they each have a numerical element: the number two occurs in v. 15a, and in vv. 7-9 the petitioner in his prayer asks for two things. Verse 15a, which is extremely obscure, may be only a fragment of a longer proverb. Its

6. There would thus be reason to suppose that this section begins with v. 11 or v. 7, were it not for the contrary evidence supplied by the LXX's arrangement of the material; (see pp. 146 n. 23, 148 above).

7. On this type of proverb, see especially Sauer, *Die Sprüche Agurs*: W.M.W. Roth, 'The Numerical Sequence x/x + 1 in the Old Testament', *VT* 12 (1962), pp. 300-11, and *Numerical Sayings in the Old Testament* (VTSup, 13; Leiden: Brill, 1965); M. Haran, 'The Graded Numerical Sequence and the Phenomenon of "Automatism" in Biblical Poetry', in G.W. Anderson *et al.* (eds.), *Congress Volume: Uppsala 1971* (VTSup, 22; Leiden: Brill, 1972), pp. 238-67; H.P. Rüger, 'Die gestaffelten Zahlensprüche des Alten Testaments und Aram. Achikar 92', *VT* 31 (1981), pp. 229-32.

position here is probably due to a common theme with vv. 15b-16: insatiability. Verse 17 is not a numerical proverb. It may have been placed here because of the occurrence of the word *nešer*, 'vulture, eagle', here and in v. 19. Similarly v. 20 about the adulteress, also not a numerical proverb, is probably intended as a comment on 'the way of a man with a girl' at the end of v. 19. Prov. 30.32-33, which has the form of an admonition, is also not a numerical proverb; but v. 33 may have been understood as mentioning two or three actions.

As far as contents are concerned, these proverbs do not appear to have been arranged in a significant order. Examples from natural phenomena (vv. 15a, 15b-16, 18-19, 24-28, 29-31) are intermingled with examples of human behaviour (vv. 11-14, 17, 20, 21-23, 32-33). In two cases (vv. 18-19, 29-31) references to animals reach a climax in the final human item.

There are different opinions among scholars as to the *purpose* of the numerical proverbs. The view that they are based on riddles in which the audience is required, simply as a game, to guess which phenomena fit a particular stated category would give them a common purpose and at the same time account for their random and miscellaneous character; but there is no evidence that this was the intention. There are, however, signs of humour in some of them, for example in vv. 21-23. Despite Van Leeuwen's thesis that this picture of the 'biblical world upside down'[8] is serious social comment and makes 'implicit appeal to the divine socio-cosmic order to quash revolutionary thoughts', at least three of the four situations described in the introduction as things which 'make the earth tremble' and under which it 'cannot bear up' turn out to be so inconsequential as to awaken a sense of the comic. There is also a touch of humour in vv. 24-28, where the final example, that of the lizard who 'is found in kings' palaces' is hardly an example of wisdom. With regard to most of the proverbs there is, perhaps, something to be said for von Rad's view that they are examples of pre-scientific attempts at the classification of phenomena: ' the counting and listing of things' which is 'an elementary need of man in his search for order';[9] but this hardly applies to them all. This is also true of the view that they are

8. R.C. Van Leeuwen, 'Proverbs 30.21-23 and the Biblical World Upside Down', *JBL* 105 (1986), pp. 599-610.
9. Von Rad, *Weisheit in Israel*, pp. 53-56 (ET pp. 35-37).

primarily concerned with teaching the importance of the acquisition of wisdom as a guide to the proper conducting of human life: this may apply to vv. 24-28, but vv. 18-19 stress the limitations of human wisdom. There is, then, little that these verses have in common beyond the fact that they are mainly, in some sense, 'numerical proverbs'. It is simply this fact that led to an editor's grouping them together.

Proverbs 31.1-9: The 'Words of King Lemuel'

These verses present no internal compositional problems. This is a unitary composition, the instruction given by the mother of a non-Israelite king, Lemuel, to her son, and thus belongs—though there is no other extant example of which the author is a woman—to the genre known as the 'royal instruction', a literary genre which appears to have been current in the ancient Near East over a very long period of time. This instruction has been compared with the Egyptian *Instruction for King Merikare* (late third millennium BC)[10] and the *Instruction of King Amenemhet* of a somewhat later date,[11] but its contents more closely resemble the Akkadian *Advice to a Prince* (probably 1000 to 700 BC).[12]

The instruction does not extend beyond v. 9; although the remainder of the chapter (vv. 10-31) has no heading of its own, its independence is shown by the fact that it is a complete alphabetic acrostic, with the initial letters of its twenty-two verses forming the Hebrew alphabet. LXX also recognized vv. 1-9 and 10-31 as independent entities, separating them by five whole chapters (25–29 in the Hebrew text). There is no reason to suppose that vv. 1-9 have undergone subsequent editing.

Proverbs 31.10-31

The literary genre known as the acrostic has been widely regarded as a latecomer to biblical literature. Acrostics—though not alphabetic ones—are, however, found in Akkadian literature, a well-known

10. English translation in *ANET*, pp. 414-18.
11. English translation in *ANET*, pp. 418-19.
12. W.G. Lambert, *Babylonian Wisdom Literature* (Oxford: Clarendon Press, 1960), pp. 110-15.

example being the co-called *Babylonian Theodicy*, probably composed about 1000 BC.[13]

Ostensibly 31.10-31 is a poem describing in extremely laudatory terms the ideal wife[14] and her activities. She is one who constantly sees to the needs of her husband, her family and her household, and works hard to maintain and increase the family's wealth and to confer honour and status on her husband. She is also acclaimed as 'a woman who fears Yahweh'. On the surface it may seem that there is no more to the poem than this, whether, as has frequently been suggested, its purpose is to list the qualities in a woman that a man ought to look for when it comes to choosing a wife, or whether it is a kind of handbook for marriageable young girls, giving them an ideal to which they must strive if they are to obtain a husband.[15] In recent years, however, an increasing number of scholars has reassessed the significance of this somewhat neglected poem, seeing the figure of the woman as in some way representing, or even as identical with, personified Wisdom herself, and the poem as constituting a climax to the whole book. These proposals, which have important implications for the question of the composition of the work as a whole, will be considered in the next chapter.

The acrostic form of the poem precludes the possibility that the text could have been subject to major editorial changes or to later scribal glosses. The only verse which has been seriously questioned is v. 30:

> Charm is deceitful, and beauty is vain,
> but a woman who fears Yahweh is to be praised.

This is the only reference to God, or to religious matters, in the poem. The second line is unusually long; and some scholars have argued that, since this is a purely 'secular' poem, this brief reference to the fear of Yahweh is incongruous and cannot be original. Gemser,

---

13. Watson, *Classical Hebrew Poetry*, pp. 191-200; Lambert, *Babylonian Wisdom Literature*, pp. 63, 67. Lambert gives a complete English translation on pp. 71-89. There is also a translation of selected parts of this work in *ANET*, pp. 438-40.

14. The expression used in v. 10 is *'ēšet ḥayil*, the same as in 12.4, where she is called 'the crown of her husband' and is contrasted with the wife who 'brings shame' (*mebîšâ*).

15. So M.B. Crook, 'The Marriageable Maiden of Prov. 31.10-31', *JNES* 13 (1954), pp. 132-40.

pointing out that the theme of choosing a suitable wife is a frequent theme in the literature of the ancient Near East,[16] suggested on the basis of the LXX (which has '*wise* woman', but *also* mentions the fear of the Lord), that the original text may have been not '*iššâ yir'at yhwh*, 'a woman who fears Yahweh', but '*ēšet bînâ*, 'a woman of understanding'. Toy and Baumgartner[17] also regarded MT as incongruous; Plöger mentioned the possibility that the whole verse in MT may have been substituted for a quite different original. Crook[18] also dismissed this slight 'colouring of religion' as a later change to the original text.

There is, however, no sufficient reason to suspect the MT here. A line of unusual length in a poem, otherwise regular in metre, can be a deliberate device to mark the conclusion of a stanza or poem, to mark a climax or for special emphasis.[19] Watson, who regards v. 30 as a tricolon (a unit of three lines rather than two), stresses the artistry with which this poem has been composed. It is divided into two parts (vv. 10-20, 21-31) consisting almost entirely of couplets; but there are two tricola. One of these occurs at the 'mathematical centre' of the first part (v. 15), while the other (v. 30) occurs almost at the end of the poem.[20]

It may plausibly be argued that v. 30, far from being no more than a token reference to religion out of keeping with the tone of the poem as a whole, is intended to form its climax. It draws attention to itself by its length, and it concludes the catalogue of the wife's virtues, summing them up in the expression 'the fear of Yahweh'. (The final

---

16. He compared the poem with a passage in the *Instruction of Ani* (*ANET*, pp. 420-21), the *Instruction of Onchsheshonqy* (B. Gemser, 'The Instruction of 'Onchsheshonqy and Biblical Wisdom Literature', in J.A. Emerton *et al.* [eds.], *Congress Volume, Oxford 1959* [VTSup, 7; Leiden: Brill, 1960], p. 129; M. Lichtheim, *Late Egyptian Wisdom Literature in the International Context: A Study of Demotic Instructions* [OBO, 52; Freiburg (Switzerland): Universitätsverlag; Göttingen: Vandenhoeck & Ruprecht, 1983], pp 49-50) and *Papyrus Insinger* 8.8-9 (Lichtheim, *Egyptian Wisdom Literature*, p. 204; cf. pp. 161-62). But a glance at these works is sufficient to show that there is no substantial similarity between them and Prov. 31.10-31.

17. W. Baumgartner, 'Die israelitische Weisheitsliteratur', *TRu* 5 (1933), p. 277.

18. 'The Marriageable Maiden', p. 137.

19. Watson, *Classical Hebrew Poetry*, p. 183.

20. Watson, *Classical Hebrew Poetry*, p. 194.

verse, urging that the woman should be given the praise which she deserves, is thus, on the thematic level, an appendix.)

The judgment that v. 30 is inappropriate in a poem entirely concerned with practical activities arises from a mistaken view that sacred and secular were two quite separate spheres in the thought of the ancient world. In this poem the ideal wife is praised almost entirely for her practical achievements; but such 'wisdom' and the 'fear of Yahweh' are constantly presented in the book of Proverbs as closely associated: in fact, true wisdom *is* the fear of Yahweh (1.7). In ch. 8 it is by wisdom that kings reign (v. 15) and wealth and prosperity are attained (v. 18). In 31.10-31, then, the ideal wife is presented as a 'wise woman' in that sense, whose practical ability is derived from her religious commitment.

Chapter 5

THE REDACTION OF THE BOOK

In the foregoing chapters an attempt has been made to trace the history of the composition of the various parts of the book of Proverbs. It is the purpose of this final chapter to investigate what can be known of the process by which the various sections were assembled and arranged to produce the book in its final form.

It is improbable that certainty can be attained in this matter. The sole *direct* textual evidence is confined to the seven headings (1.1; 10.1; 22.17; 24.23; 25.1; 30.1; 31.1) which serve to mark divisions of the book in MT, together with the differences both of arrangement and of headings between MT and LXX.[1]

In general it may be said that the book of Proverbs was compiled as a compendium of traditional educational or instructional material in order to gather on to a single scroll all writings of this kind which the final editor thought should be preserved. If the headings at 30.1 and 31.1 indicate, as they appear to do, that the verses which follow are of non-Israelite origin, this editor did not narrowly restrict the scope of his work entirely to the wisdom of his own people, but included— though placing it near the end of the book—material from elsewhere.[2]

---

1. The only substantial differences between MT's and LXX's headings are that LXX lacks a heading altogether at 10.1; that at 24.23 LXX has, 'And this I say to you that are wise, to learn'; and that at both 30.1 and 31.1 the names Agur son of Jakeh and Lemuel are lacking in LXX. LXX has no heading at 30.1, and at 31.1 it reads, 'My words have been spoken by God. An oracle of a king, whom his mother instructed.' In all these cases the text of MT is the more original; this is especially evident at 30.1 and 31.1, where it is more likely that LXX should have suppressed the names than that MT should have introduced such 'outlandish' names. For the different *arrangement* of the sections in LXX see p. 146 n. 23 above.

2. The places of origin of Agur and Lemuel are not certain. The word *maśśā'* in 30.1 (*hammaśśā'* in 31.1) may be the name of a place or district (*hammaśśā'* has

As has been demonstrated in the foregoing chapters, the book is composed of a number of originally distinct sections, of which the majority have had more or less complicated histories of their own. These sections originated and developed in different social circles and at different times, and comprise a number of quite different literary forms. Despite this, they have much in common apart from a common didactic purpose: there are also a number of themes running through much of the book. These include the importance of the acquisition of wisdom; the absolute contrast between the wise and foolish and between the righteous and wicked, and the respective fates of these; the need to choose the right path, and the consequences of doing or failing to do this. There are also recurring topics such as the power of the spoken word for good or evil, especially the power of persuasion. Another persistent feature is a preoccupation with female figures; estimable wives and disgraceful wives, the queen mother, mothers who share the teaching of their children with their husbands, the personified figures of Wisdom and Folly, the prostitute and the adulteress. All these features combine to give the book a kind of unity which can hardly be entirely accidental, and has suggested to some scholars that there has been some degree of interaction between the various parts of the book.[3]

There is, however, no evidence of a systematic editing of the whole book for dogmatic or theological reasons. Although some passages (especially some of the instructions in chs. 1–9 and some passages in 10.1–22.16) have been expanded with references to Yahweh as creator, arbiter of human conduct, source of rewards and punishments

---

been emended by some scholars to *hammaśśā'î*, 'the Massaite'), so RSV, NEB, JB, REB; but it may mean '(the) oracle' (so NRSV). A footnote in JB identifies it with an Ishmaelite tribe of North Arabia on the basis of Gen. 25.14; but a place in Edom has also been suggested. 1 Kgs 4.30 (Heb. 5.10) knows of 'the wisdom of the people of the east' and also that of Egypt.

3.   T.P. McCreesh, 'Wisdom as Wife: Proverbs 31.10-31', *RB* 92 (1985), pp. 25-46; C.V. Camp, *Wisdom and the Feminine in the Book of Proverbs* (Sheffield: Almond Press, 1985), pp. 186-208. For example, commenting on a possible relationship between chs. 1–9 and 31 on the one hand and 23.22–24.4 on the other, Camp (p. 201) argues that 'a conscious editorial effort was made to include within the body of the proverb collection a unit of instruction material that correspond to the thematic pattern being developed at the beginning and end of the book of Proverbs'.

and so on, there are surprisingly large parts of the book where there are no references to Yahweh—or to 'God'—at all. It is therefore not possible to postulate a 'Yahweh-redaction' of the book by a final editor. The same may be said of the representation of wisdom in personal terms. This is found only in chs. 1–9—a relatively small section of the book—and even there only in 1.20-33, 8.1-36 and in a few of the instructions.[4] There is no trace of it in the prologue, 1.1-7.

Proverbs 1–9 and 31.10-31: The Framework

Nevertheless, it may be said with some confidence that there is a correspondence between the first and last sections of the book (chs. 1–9 and 31), which is a major structural feature and provides the book with a framework within which the various intervening elements can take their place, and which sets the tone that the final editor wished to give to it. This structural feature has been recognized by a number of recent scholars.[5] It has been observed that the opening and/or closing of a number of Old Testament books are particularly significant as indicating the way in which final editors intended those books to be read. This is true, for example, of the opening and final chapters of Deuteronomy, perhaps of Joshua 24, of Ruth 4.18-22, of 2 Kgs 25.27-30, of the final section of Esther, possibly of the prologue and epilogue of Job, of Psalm 1 (or 1–2), of Eccl. 12.9-13, of Hos. 14.9 and possibly of some other of the prophetical books.

It is perhaps significant that 31.10-31, though it is obviously demarcated by its acrostic form, is the only section of the book to lack a heading: this may suggest that it was appended to the book by an editor different from, or subsequent to, the editor who assembled 10.1–31.9. As will be shown below, this final editor was familiar with chs. 1–9 in more or less their present form.

4. Prov. 14.1, if the common emendation of the first line of that verse to 'Wisdom has built her house' is correct (see p. 100 n. 31 above), appears to be an exception.

5. Especially Camp, *Wisdom and the Feminine*, pp. 183-91; McCreesh, 'Wisdom as Wife'; Meinhold, *Die Sprüche* (p. 26). Others, including E. Jacob ('Sagesse et alphabet. A propos de Proverbes 31.10-31', in A. Caquot and M. Philonenko (eds.), *Hommages à André Dupont-Sommer* [Paris: Librairie d'Amérique et d'Orient Adrien-Maisonneuve, 1971], p. 291) recognize the significance of 31.10-31 in this connection.

The choice of the alphabetic acrostic for this poem is significant. While there are different views about the function of the alphabetic acrostic as it appears in the Old Testament—there are at least fifteen examples of it[6]—and these are not necessarily mutually exclusive,[7] there is now considerable agreement that a main purpose, if not the only one, was to convey the notion of totality or completeness.[8] This is especially plausible in the case of Prov. 31.10-31, which not only completes the book of Proverbs but also comprises such a comprehensive list of virtues that it might be said to be intended to constitute in itself a compendium of all human wisdom.

Is the portrayal of the wife in 31.10-31 primarily symbolic, or is it presented as a description of a real, if idealized, wife? In other words, is she intended to represent Wisdom herself? Certain features of the text have been thought to suggest that the writer at least intended the reader to find in the poem echoes of the figure of Wisdom in chs. 1–9.[9] Wolters[10] saw in the word *ṣôpiyyâ*, 'She watches over (sc. the ways of her household)', v. 27, a pun on the Greek word *sophia*, 'wisdom', dating the poem in the Greek period. Others[11] have pointed out that *yir'at* in v. 30, generally regarded as an irregular form of the *qal* participle construct of the verb *yārē'* 'to fear' so that the whole phrase *'iššâ yir'at yhwh* would mean 'a woman who fears Yahweh', is also the regular form of the feminine construct of the noun *yir'â*, 'fear', so that the whole phrase could mean 'a woman (who *is*) the fear of Yahweh'.

6.   W.G.E. Watson, *Classical Hebrew Poetry: A Guide to its Techniques* (JSOTSup, 26; Sheffield: JSOT Press, 1984), p. 192.

7.   Watson, *Classical Hebrew Poetry*, pp. 197-99, refers to the main theories: that the purpose was to aid memory, that it was to teach the alphabet, that it was to symbolize or give the impression of completeness or totality, or that it was to demonstrate the skill of the writer. He regarded the last two of these as the most probable.

8.   So, e.g., N.K. Gottwald, *Studies in the Book of Lamentations* (SBT, 14; London: SCM Press, 1954), pp. 24-32; Jacob, 'Sagesse et alphabet', pp. 290-91; Watson, *Classical Hebrew Poetry*, p. 197.

9.   A. Barucq, *Le livre des Proverbes* (SB; Paris: Gabalda, 1964), p. 231 states that the figure is 'une forme de sagesse' and that the poem is to be seen as parallel to the depiction of Wisdom in 9.1-6.

10.   A. Wolters, '*Ṣôpiyyā* (Prov. 31.27) as Hymnic Participle and Play on Sophia', *JBL* 104 (1985), pp. 577-87.

11.   E.g. E. Jacob, 'Sagesse et alphabet', p. 294.

However this may be, the affinities between chs. 1–9 and 31.10-31 are unmistakable. Whereas in 10.1–31.9 the word *'iššâ* (woman) occurs only thirteen times, in chs. 1–9 more than half of the total number of verses (256) are concerned in one way or another with female figures: with mother, bride, wife, adulteress, prostitute, personified Wisdom and Folly. This proportion is unequalled in any book of the Old Testament with the exception of Ruth and the Song of Songs. It cannot be coincidence that the final section of the book should be entirely devoted to a female figure.

Another remarkable feature linking these chapters is that, in contrast to most of the other books of the Old Testament, these female figures are the active and dominant ones compared with their partners. In 31.10-31 the husband plays a very minor, if distinguished, role (vv. 11-12, 23, 28), while it is the wife who enhances the family's wealth and prestige, not only seeing to the needs and wellbeing of her husband, children and servants, but maintaining a successful cottage industry and even buying a field and planting a vineyard. It is also of significance that the setting is a domestic one.[12] In 9.1 Wisdom builds her house; in 31.10-31 the house is already happily and successfully established: the promise of chs. 1–9 has been fulfilled and completed.

In chs. 1–9 Wisdom is presented as a teacher (8.14); the wife in the final poem is also a teacher who 'opens her mouth with wisdom' (v. 26). She stands for stability—in contrast with the adulteress and the woman Folly who are ignorant and unstable (5.6; 7.11; 9.13).

The opening line of the poem, 'Who can find a capable wife?' (*'ēšet-ḥayil mî yimṣā'*, 31.10a) expresses what was evidently a commonplace concern in ancient Israel (compare, e.g., Prov. 12.4; 18.22); but in a wider sense the verb *māṣā'* 'to find' represents a major topic in chs. 1–9, where no less than five verses (1.28; 3.13; 4.22; 8.17, 35) refer to the importance of 'finding' Wisdom and her teaching. Those who find her are pronounced 'happy', and it is promised that they will 'find' life. On the other hand, *māṣā'* is used of the adulteress; but it is she who there takes the initiative and sets out to find the young man, to his destruction (7.15). In 31.10-31 the manifold benefits conferred on the man who finds the *'ēšet-ḥayil* are

---

12. The word 'house' (*bayit*) occurs four times: vv. 15, 21 (twice), 27; *nᵉ'ārôt*, 'maidservants' in v. 15; children (*bānîm*) in v. 28.

set out in every detail. Like Wisdom (3.15; 8.11) she is 'far more precious than jewels' (31.10b) and incomparable.

The Intermediate Sections

Camp[13] argues not only that there are close affinities between chs. 1–9 and 31.10-31 and that these two sections of the book form a framework to the rest, but also that they were deliberately composed in order to develop and reinterpret the themes and images of chs. 10–29. The final editor of the book encapsulated the proverb collections within this specially constructed envelope, so causing the whole to express his own view of the nature of wisdom: he chose (or composed) the poems as specifically developing themes and topics that occur in chs. 10–29 in a new way, giving the book a unified character.[14]

Among the examples which Camp gives of such an intention is the building by Wisdom of her house (14.1). Another is the imagery of the crown (*ʿaṭārâ*) which is bestowed by Wisdom (4.9): she compares this with 12.4, 14.24, 16.31 and 17.6 in which the word *ʿaṭārâ* occurs—but only two of these verses are in fact comparable with 4.9. Prov. 14.24a, 'The crown of the wise is their wisdom' (not in MT, but conjectured from LXX) may be relevant to her argument, and 12.4a, 'A capable wife (*ēšet-ḥayil*) is the crown of her husband' could be regarded as the kernel of the poem in 31.10-31, although the word 'crown' does not actually occur in that poem. Other topics held by Camp to be relevant to her theme are the thought of Wisdom as incomparably precious (2.4; 3.14-15; 8.10-11, 19; cf. 20.15 and 31.10b) and the image of the tree of life (*ʿēṣ ḥayyîm*, 11.30; 13.12; 15.4) which occurs also in 3.18. Only in 3.18, however, is the phrase used of Wisdom.

Camp's contention is that 'Wisdom and folly, righteousness and wickedness, those two fundamental dichotomies of the proverbs, are personified and epitomized in the introductory poems' of chs. 1–9.[15] This may well be so in a general way, and it may also be true of 31.10-31, where the wife embodies so many of the traits of Wisdom.

---

13. *Wisdom and the Feminine*, pp. 191-208.
14. It is noteworthy that she appears to be unable to fit ch. 30 into this scheme.
15. *Wisdom and the Feminine*, p. 191.

But the examples that Camp offers of specific literary connections between these chapters and the proverb collections are less convincing: more allowance needs to be made for the existence of a common stock of topics and expressions to which all the authors of the book of Proverbs had access. This would include the standard language proper to parental education that is found in a number of proverbs as well as in the instructions of chs. 1–9. The 'instructions' in chs. 10–29 are neither imitations nor precursors of the instruction form in chs. 1–9; these are *parallel*, not sequential, phenomena. It seems to be the case that the final editors of the book had only a general intention to preserve within their framework all those collections of wisdom teaching known to them that they considered worth preserving. As regards the final composition of the book, then, the problem that remains is when and how these intervening sections were assembled in the order in which we now have them, and on what principle, if any, the compilation was made.[16]

The evidence is meagre. The only palpable clues are to be found in the headings of the various sections and in the differences in the order of those sections in MT and LXX. If it were possible to give approximate dates to the individual sections this could well have a bearing on the history of redaction; but for the most part this is not possible. The only reasonably secure dating of any section is the reference to the activity of Hezekiah's scribes in 25.1 together with the word 'also' in the same verse. This probably implies that the two 'Solomonic' collections, 10.1–22.16 and 25–29, were formed during the period of the monarchy, the latter during the later monarchy. It is possible that these two sections formed the nucleus of the book. However, if this is so, it is difficult to explain why the LXX separates them so completely from one another.

Despite much argument to the contrary, it is not possible to date different parts of the book by their contents, point of view, theology

16. I am unable to accept the view of P.W. Skehan in 'Wisdom's House', *CBQ* 29 (1967), pp. 162-80; and 'A Single Editor for the Whole Book of Proverbs', *CBQ* 10 (1948), pp. 115-30 (republished in revised form in *Studies in Israelite Poetry and Wisdom* [CBQMS, 1; Washington, DC; Catholic Biblical Association of America, 1971], pp. 27-45 and 15-26 respectively), which is based on the idea of the book as having the architectural form of Solomon's Temple and on various mathematical calculations such as the numerical values of the names 'Solomon' and 'Hezekiah'.

or literary form.[17] It is now well known that the individual short proverb and the longer wisdom poem were two distinctive genres which continued to be employed simultaneously in the ancient Near East from early until quite late times;[18] one is not derived from the other. It has been shown above that the proverb collections in the book have been edited to form cohesive 'instructions'; but, as has also been pointed out, it is improbable that these loosely formed 'instructions' were in some sense imitations of the kind of instruction found in chs. 1–9: there is probably no literary connection between the two phenomena. The view that one can trace an intermediate development in the literary wisdom tradition from the simple and 'primitive' to the complex and sophisticated is also extremely improbable. The discussion by Lichtheim[19] of the variety of forms of Egyptian wisdom literature shows how diverse are the literary types that can be so labelled in the ancient Near Eastern traditions, and how each type had its own *raison d'être* determined by scribal and other factors which, at least in the case of Israel, are unknown to us.

The headings to the sections in MT (apart from 1.1)[20] may provide some clue to their original arrangement:

10.1	Proverbs (*mišᵉlê*) of Solomon
22.17	Words (*dibᵉrê*) of wise men (*hᵃkāmîm*).
24.23	These also are of wise men (*hᵃkāmîm*).

---

17. Such a view has been very widely held. It is still maintained by some scholars, e.g. H.D. Preuss, *Einführung in die alttestamentliche Weisheitsliteratur* (Stuttgart, Kohlhammer, 1987), pp. 60-61.

18. Two examples of late works composed of short 'monostichs' are the Egyptian demotic works, *The Instruction of Ankhsheshonqy* and *The Instruction of Papyrus Insinger*, both written in the Hellenistic period: see M. Lichtheim, *Late Egyptian Wisdom Literature in the International Context: A Study of Demotic Instructions* (Freiburg [Switzerland]: Universitätsverlag; Göttingen: Vandenhoeck & Ruprecht, 1983). On the other hand, on a pre-exilic date for chs. 1–9 postulated on the analogy of comparable Egyptian works of a relatively early period, see especially C. Kayatz, *Studien zu Proverbien 1–9* (WMANT, 22; Neukirchen–Vluyn: Neukirchener Verlag, 1966), pp. 4, 10, 135-39; compare also H. Brunner, *Altägyptische Weisheit: Lehren für das Leben* (Zürich: Artemis Verlag, 1988), pp. 45-61 on the history of the Egyptian instruction and B. Lang, *Wisdom and the Book of Proverbs: An Israelite Goddess Redefined* (New York: Pilgrim Press, 1986), pp. 4-12.

19. Lichtheim, *Late Egyptian Wisdom Literature*, pp. 1-12.

20. On this verse see pp. 53 above.

25.1	These also are proverbs (*miš^elê*) of Solomon that...
30.1	Words (*dib^erê*) of Agur...
31.1	Words (*dib^erê*) of King Lemuel...

A deliberate distinction thus appears to have been made between 'proverbs (of Solomon)' and 'words (of wise men, Agur, Lemuel)'. The sections belonging to the first group are longer than those in the latter group, and it is reasonable to see the latter as secondary additions to the two major collections of proverbs. The apparently non-Israelite origin of the Agur and Lemuel sections and their relegation to the end of the book may be a further indication of their secondary character (so Plöger). The use of the word 'also' (*gam-*) at 25.1, however, may suggest a somewhat different original order in which one collection of 'Solomonic' proverbs once immediately followed the other.

The different order in which the sections are arranged in LXX after 24.22 has never been plausibly accounted for. The opinion has been expressed that these chapters had not attained a fixed order when the book was translated into Greek (probably in the first century BC). This is possible; but the more logical arrangement in MT is probably the more original. It is not known why LXX has a different order.

From what has been said above it must be admitted that there is insufficient evidence to uncover the whole process by which the different sections of the book came to be arranged in their present order, although there are some partial indications. Undoubtedly the process was a complex one: there were partial 'editions' before the final one in which those collections which already existed were gathered together within the framework constituted by chs. 1–9 and 31.10-31.

SELECT BIBLIOGRAPHY

Aletti, J.-N., 'Séduction et parole en Proverbes I–IX', *VT* 27 (1977), pp. 129-44.

Barucq, A., *Le livre des Proverbes* (SB; Paris: Gabalda, 1964).

Bauer-Kayatz, C., *Einführung in die alttestamentliche Weisheit* (Biblische Studien, 55; Neukirchen–Vluyn: Neukirchener Verlag, 1969).

Baumgartner, W., 'Die israelitische Weisheitsliteratur', *TRu* 5 (1933), pp. 259-88.

Boström, G., *Paronomasi i den äldre hebreiska Maschallitteraturen med särskild hänsyn till Proverbia* (LUÅ, NS I/23/8; Lund: Gleerup; Leipzig: Otto Harrassowitz, 1928).

Brunner, H., *Altägyptische Weisheit: Lehren für das Leben* (Zürich: Artemis Verlag, 1988).

Bryce, G.E., 'Another Wisdom-"Book" in Proverbs', *JBL* 91 (1972), pp. 145-57.

—*A Legacy of Wisdom: The Egyptian Contribution to the Wisdom of Israel* (Lewisburg: Bucknell University Press; London: Associated University Presses, 1979).

Camp, C.V., *Wisdom and the Feminine in the Book of Proverbs* (Sheffield: Almond Press, 1985).

Cowley, A.E., *Aramaic Papyri of the Fifth Century B.C.* (Oxford: Clarendon Press, 1923).

Crook, M.B., 'The Marriageable Maiden of Prov. 31.10-31', *JNES* 13 (1954), pp. 132-40.

Driver, S.R., *A Treatise on the Use of the Tenses in Hebrew* (Oxford: Clarendon Press, 1892).

Eissfeldt, O., *Der Maschal im Alten Testament* (BZAW, 24; Giessen: Töpelmann, 1913).

Erman, A., 'Eine ägyptische Quelle der "Sprüche Salomos"', *SPAW* 15 (1924), pp. 86-93.

Franklyn, P., 'The Sayings of Agur in Proverbs 30: Piety or Scepticism?', *ZAW* 95 (1983), pp. 238-52.

Gemser, B., *Sprüche Salomos* (HAT, 16; Tübingen: Mohr, 1937; 2nd edn, 1963).

—'The Importance of the Motive Clause in Old Testament Law', in G.W. Anderson *et al.* (eds.), *Congress Volume: Copenhagen 1953* (VTSup, 1; Leiden: Brill, 1953), pp. 50-66.

Gilbert, M., 'Le discours de la sagesse en Proverbes, 8. Structure et cohérence', in M. Gilbert (ed.), *La sagesse de l'Ancien Testament* (BETL, 51; Leuven: Leuven University Press, 1979), pp. 202-18.

—'Le discours menaçant de sagesse en Proverbes 1.20-33', in D. Garrone and F. Israel (eds.), *Storia e tradizioni di Israele: Scritti in onore di J. Alberto Soggin* (Brescia: Paideia, 1991), pp. 99-119.

Goldingay, J.E., 'Proverbs V and IX', *RB* 84 (1977), pp. 80-93.

Golka, F.W., 'Die israelitische Weisheitsschule oder "des Kaisers neue Kleider"', *VT* 33 (1983), pp. 257-71.

Gordon, E.I., *Sumerian Proverbs: Glimpses of Everyday Life in Ancient Mesopotamia* (New York: Greenwood Press, 1968).

Gottwald, N.K., *Studies in the Book of Lamentations* (SBT, 14; London: SCM Press, 1954).

Griffith, F.L., 'The Teaching of Amenophis, the Son of Kanekht', *JEA* 12 (1926), pp. 191-231.

Haran, M., 'The Graded Numerical Sequence and the Phenomenon of "Automatism" in Biblical Poetry', in G.W. Anderson *et al.* (eds.), *Congress Volume: Uppsala 1971* (VTSup, 22; Leiden: Brill, 1972), pp. 238-67.

Hermisson, H.-J., *Studien zur israelitischen Spruchweisheit* (WMANT, 28; Neukirchen–Vluyn: Neukirchener Verlag, 1968).

Hildebrandt, T., 'Proverbial Pairs: Compositional Units in Proverbs 10–29', *JBL* 107 (1988), pp. 207-24.

Humbert, P., 'La "femme étrangère" du livre des Proverbes', *RES* 6 (1937), pp. 49-64.

—'Les adjectifs "zâr" et "nokrî" et la "femme étrangère" des proverbes bibliques', in *Mélanges syriens offerts à M. René Dussaud* (Paris: Paul Geuthner, 1939), I, pp. 159-66 = *Opuscules d'un hébraïsant* (Neuchâtel: Delachaux & Niestlé, 1958), pp. 111-18.

Jacob, E., 'Sagesse et alphabet. A propos de Proverbes 31.10-31', in *Hommages à André Dupont-Sommer* (Paris: Librairie d'Amérique et d'Orient Adrien-Maisonnneuve, 1971), pp. 287-95.

Kayatz, C., *Studien zu Proverbien 1–9* (WMANT, 22; Neukirchen–Vluyn: Neukirchener Verlag, 1966).

Kitchen, K.A., 'Egypt and Israel during the First Millennium B.C.', in J.A. Emerton (ed.), *Congress Volume: Jerusalem 1986* (VTSup, 40; Leiden: Brill, 1988), pp. 107-23.

Krispenz, J., *Spruchkompositionen im Buch Proverbia* (Europäische Hochschulschriften, 349; Frankfurt: Peter Lang, 1989).

Lambert, W.G., *Babylonian Wisdom Literature* (Oxford: Clarendon Press, 1960).

Lang, B., *Die weisheitliche Lehrrede: Eine Untersuchung von Sprüche 1–7* (SBS, 54; Stuttgart: KBW, 1972).

—*Frau Weisheit: Deutung einer biblischen Gestalt* (Düsseldorf: Patmos, 1975).

—'Schule und Unterricht im alten Israel', in M. Gilbert (ed.), *'La Sagesse de l'Ancien Testament* (BETL, 51; Leuven: Leuven University Press, 1979), pp. 186-201.

—*Wisdom and the Book of Proverbs: An Israelite Goddess Redefined* (New York: Pilgrim Press, 1986).

Lemaire, A., *Les écoles et la formation de la Bible dans l'ancien Israël* (OBO, 39; Fribourg [Switzerland]: Editions Universitaires; Göttingen: Vandenhoeck & Ruprecht, 1981).

Lichtheim, M., *Late Egyptian Wisdom Literature in the International Context: A Study of Demotic Instructions* (OBO, 52; Freiburg [Switzerland]: Universitätsverlag; Göttingen: Vandenhoeck & Ruprecht, 1983).

McCreesh, T.P., 'Wisdom as Wife: Proverbs 31.10-31', *RB* 92 (1985), pp. 25-46.

McKane, W., *Proverbs: A New Approach* (OTL; London: SCM Press, 1970).

Meinhold, A., *Die Sprüche*. I. *Sprüche Kapital 1–15* (Zürcher Kommentare AT, 16.1; Zürich: Theologischer Verlag, 1991).

168 The Composition of the Book of Proverbs

Niccacci, A., 'Proverbi 22.17–23.11', *Studii Biblici Franciscani Liber Annuus* (Jerusalem) 29 (1979), pp. 42-72.

Plöger, O., 'Zur Auslegung der Sentenzensammlungen des Proverbiabuches', in H.W. Wolff (ed.), *Probleme biblischer Theologie: Gerhard von Rad zum 70. Geburtstag* (Munich: Kaiser Verlag, 1971), pp. 402-16.

—*Sprüche Salomos (Proverbia)* (BKAT, 17; Neukirchen–Vluyn: Neukirchener Verlag, 1984).

Preuss, H.D., *Einführung in die alttestamentliche Weisheitsliteratur* (Stuttgart: Kohlhammer, 1987).

Rad, G. von, *Weisheit in Israel* (Neukirchen–Vluyn: Neukirchener Verlag, 1970). ET *Wisdom in Israel* (London: SCM Press, 1972).

Renfroe, F., 'The Effect of Redaction on the Structure of Prov. 1.1-6', *ZAW* 101 (1989), pp. 290-93.

Richter, W., *Recht und Ethos: Versuch einer Ortung des weisheitlichen Mahnspruches* (SANT, 15; Munich: Kösel, 1966).

Ringgren, H., *Sprüche Salomos* (ATD, 16; Göttingen: Vandenhoeck & Ruprecht, 2nd edn, 1967 [1962]).

Römheld, D., *Wege der Weisheit: Die Lehren Amenemopes und Proverbien 22,17–24,22* (BZAW, 184; Berlin: de Gruyter, 1989).

Roth, W.M.W., 'The Numerical Sequence x/x + 1 in the Old Testament', *VT* 12 (1962), pp. 300-11.

—*Numerical Sayings in the Old Testament* (VTSup, 13; Leiden: Brill, 1965).

Rüger, H.P., 'Die gestaffelten Zahlensprüche des Alten Testaments und Aram. Achikar 92', *VT* 31 (1981), pp. 229-34.

Ruffle, J., 'The Teaching of Amenemope and its Connection with the Book of Proverbs', *TynBul* 28 (1977), pp. 29-68.

Sauer, G., *Die Sprüche Agurs: Untersuchungen zur Herkunft, Verbreitung und Bedeutung einer biblischer Stilform unter besonderer Berücksichtigung von Proverbia c. 30* (BWANT, 84: Stuttgart: Kohlhammer, 1963).

Scott, R.B.Y., *Proverbs/Ecclesiastes* (AB, 18: New York: Doubleday, 1965).

Skehan, P.W., 'A Single Editor for the Whole Book of Proverbs', *CBQ* 10 (1948), pp. 115-30 = *Studies in Israelite Poetry and Wisdom* (CBQMS, 1; Washington, DC: Catholic Biblical Association of America, rev. edn, 1971), pp. 15-26.

—Wisdom's House', *CBQ* 29 (1967), pp. 162-80 = *Studies in Israelite Poetry and Wisdom*, pp. 27-45.

Skladny, U., *Die ältesten Spruchsammlungen in Israel* (Göttingen: Vandenhoeck & Ruprecht, 1962).

Snijders, L.A., 'The Meaning of *zâr* in the Old Testament. An Exegetical Study', *OTS* 10 (1954), pp. 1-154.

Thompson, J.M., *The Form and Function of Proverbs in Ancient Israel* (The Hague: Mouton, 1974).

Torrey, C.C., 'Proverbs, Chapter 30', *JBL* 73 (1954), pp. 93-96.

Toy, C.H., *Proverbs* (ICC; Edinburgh: T. & T. Clark, 1899).

Van Leeuwen, R.C., 'Proverbs 30.21-23 and the Biblical World Upside Down', *JBL* 105 (1986), pp. 599-610.

—*Context and Meaning in Proverbs 25–27* (SBLDS, 96; Atlanta: Scholars Press, 1988).

Watson, W.G.E., *Classical Hebrew Poetry: A Guide to its Techniques* (JSOTSup, 26; Sheffield: JSOT Press, 1984).

Westermann, C., 'Weisheit im Sprichwort', in K.-H. Bernhardt (ed.), *Schalom: Studien zu Glaube und Geschichte Israels, Alfred Jepsen zum 70. Geburtstag* (Stuttgart: Calwer Verlag, 1971), pp. 73-85, = *Forschung am Alten Testament: Gesammelte Studien* (TBü, Altes Testament, 55; Munich: Chr. Kaiser Verlag, 1974), II, pp. 149-61.

—*Wurzeln der Weisheit: Die ältesten Sprüche Israels und anderer Völker* (Göttingen: Vandenhoeck & Ruprecht, 1990).

Whybray, R.N., 'The Concept of Wisdom in Proverbs I–IX' (DPhil Thesis, University of Oxford, 1962).

—*Wisdom in Proverbs* (SBT, 45; London: SCM Press, 1965).

—'Some Literary Problems in Proverbs I–IX', *VT* 16 (1966), pp. 482-96.

—*The Intellectual Tradition in the Old Testament* (BZAW, 135; Berlin: de Gruyter, 1974).

—'Yahweh-Sayings and their Contexts in Proverbs 10,1–22,16', in M. Gilbert (ed.), *La sagesse de l'Ancien Testament* (BETL, 51; Gembloux Duculot; Leuven: Leuven University Press, 1979), pp. 153-65.

—*Wealth and Poverty in the Book of Proverbs* (JSOTSup, 99; Sheffield: JSOT Press, 1990).

—'Thoughts on the Composition of Proverbs 10–29', in E. Ulrich *et al.* (eds.), *Priests, Prophets and Scribes: Essays on the Formation and Heritage of Second Temple Judaism in Honour of Joseph Blenkinsopp* (JSOTSup, 149; Sheffield: JSOT Press, 1992), pp. 102-14.

Williams, R.J., *Hebrew Syntax: An Outline* (Toronto: Toronto University Press, 1967).

Wolters, A., '*Šôpiyyâ* (Prov. 31.27) as Hymnic Participle and Play on *Sophia*', *JBL* 104 (1985), pp. 577-87.

—'Proverbs xxxi 10-31 as Heroic Hymn: A Form-Critical Analysis', *VT* 38 (1988), pp. 446-57.

INDEX OF AUTHORS

JOURNAL FOR THE STUDY OF THE OLD TESTAMENT

Supplement Series